third edition

Views
and Values

Diverse Readings
on Universal Themes

Kari Sayers

Marymount College

THOMSON

──── ✳ ────™

WADSWORTH

Australia   Canada   Mexico   Singapore   Spain   United Kingdom   United States

Views and Values: Diverse Readings on Universal Themes
Third Edition
Kari Sayers

Publisher: *Michael Rosenberg*
Acquisitions Editor: *Stephen Dalphin*
Editorial Assistant: *Stephen Marsi*
Associate Production Project Manager: *Karen Stocz*
Technology Project Manager: *Joe Gallagher*
Marketing Manager: *Carrie Brandon*
Associate Marketing Manager: *Joe Piazza*
Senior Print Buyer: *Mary Beth Hennebury*
Composition/Project Management: *Thompson Steele, Inc.*
Text Design: *Thompson Steele, Inc.*
Cover Designer: *Gina Petti/Rotunda*
Printer: *Malloy Lithographing*

Printed in the United States of America
2 3 4 5 6 7 09 08 07 06 05

For more information about our products, contact us at:
Thomson Learning Academic Resource Center
1-800-423-0563
For permission to use material from this text or product, submit a
request online at **http://www.thomsonrights.com.**
Any additional questions about permissions can be submitted by
email to **thomsonrights@thomson.com.**

Library of Congress Control Number: 2004102713

ISBN 0-8384-0777-3

Thematic Contents

Men and Women—Love and Relationships   55

Guilt and Innocence   93

Myths, Legends, and Tales   169

Race, Culture, and Identity   197

Contents
by Country

To the Instructor

In line with the theory that reading and writing students need a variety of reading material, not only short essays but longer pieces with more depth, this latest edition of *Views and Values* continues to provide students with excellent literary selections from our classical heritage, both fiction and nonfiction, that require some scrutiny and analysis. Because of some teachers' recommendations, we have replaced a couple of the least popular stories with three new short stories and an essay: "A Man Who Had No Eyes" by MacKinlay Kantor, "The Beggarwoman of Locarno" by Heinrich von Kleist, "Harrison Bergeron" by Kurt Vonnegut, Jr., and "Fresh Air Will Kill You" by Art Buchwald.

As before, the objective of this book is to develop not only reading and writing skills but also the ability to think critically. Students will be exposed to excellent literature by prize-winning authors from around the world, beautifully written short fiction and nonfiction with real depth, stories that make students feel and experience events with well-drawn characters, and stories that invite students to think about important values in their own daily lives.

Yet, even though the stories have been chosen for their high literary quality, they have also been chosen for their relative brevity and accessibility. Whether old or new, all the stories make simple statements about the human condition that today's students can easily understand and relate to.

Apparatus

Preceding each story are a few broad, open-ended questions that are meant to motivate the students to read and to create a "hook" for the students to hang the story on. Instructors may, of course, pose more questions of their own. A simple glossary also precedes most stories.

Following each story are comprehension and discussion questions. The questions are not separated into independent skills because it has been our experience that reading skills cannot always be neatly divided into separate categories. Nevertheless, instructors will recognize such skills as focusing on important details that make up the main point; making inferences; drawing conclusions; sequencing; detecting an author's bias and tone as well as a story's mood; appreciating style; evaluating evidence; and making judgments. However, the questions have been grouped into broader categories such as recalling, interpreting, and evaluating. Many poor readers lack the ability to visualize what they read. By constantly asking them to focus on description and plot details, this important skill will improve. Similarly, by repeated practice with questions that require interpreting and evaluating, students develop critical thinking skills that will carry over to reading other types of prose as well as to their own writing. Some instructors may prefer to assign only these more open-ended questions.

Also following each story are several writing topics either based on the story itself or related to a theme in the story. Some topics lend themselves to paragraph practice, whereas other topics are broader and may be better developed in essays as indicated. Suggested thesis statements are included as a starting point for discussion and writing, but are not meant to preclude other ways of developing a particular topic.

An instructor's manual with possible answers to the comprehension questions is available. Included in the instructor's manual is also a suggestion for a different way to group the stories other than by thematic content, multiple-choice questions and true/false quick-check tests, as well as sample paragraphs and essays written by students in response to the writing topics. Although this reader is intended as a supplement to a core reading skills or writing textbook, we have included a summary of the most frequently taught reading strategies and the most common points of the writing process for those who choose to teach without a core text.

Finally, the reading level of each story has been measured using the Fry method and recorded in the manual.

Acknowledgments

I wish to thank my colleagues and students at Marymount College for their ideas and encouragement. Special thanks to Ottillie Boboc, Joan Cashion, Mary Beth Culp, Lisa DeNiscia, Belle Levinson-Brubaker, Greg Levonian, Al Lewis, Lynn McLeod, Francie Miller, Ruth Proctor, Nancy Sanders, Bruce Schwartz, Eileen Smith, Charles Spurgeon, Kathy Vertullo, and Rhonda Wiley.

Furthermore, I wish to extend my appreciation to the many reviewers for their excellent recommendations and suggestions:

Dorothy Dobbins, Bethune-Cookman College

Carol A. Galbus, Winona State University

Peggy Harbors, Nashville State Tech

Shelly Hedstrom, Palm Beach Community College

Gary Kay, Broward Community College, South Campus

Mark Medvetz, University of Montana at Missoula

Geraldine Gaugherty, University of Southern Colorado

Marilyn Kay Trentham, DeKalb Technical Institute

Karen O'Donnell, Finger Lakes Community College

Suzanne Crawford, Saddleback College.

I am also grateful to Chris Caperton and Steve Dalphin along with the editors and assistants at Wadsworth for their professional yet friendly approach to publishing.

Finally, I want to thank my husband for his endless patience, support, and love.

To the Student

If you want to improve your reading and writing skills, this book is for you. Of course, being a college student you probably think you read and write fairly well, but may lack some vocabulary and grammar skills for advanced work. While having good vocabulary and grammar skills is essential to both reading and writing, equally important is clear thinking. In addition to developing your vocabulary and sentence structure, this book, then, will develop your ability to think clearly and critically about what you have read so that you can get ready to write. While practicing your reading and writing skills, you will also meet characters from different places and backgrounds, experience their problems and pleasures, and learn from their mistakes. Welcome to the wonderful world of literature!

Before you start reading, take a moment to reflect on the questions preceding each story and look over the vocabulary. Then read the story carefully, preferably in one sitting, and answer the comprehension questions after the story. Finally, try to relate the events in the stories to your own life by focusing on the topics for writing and further discussion.

To familiarize yourself with this book, look at the Contents. How are the stories arranged in the Contents? What are some of the general themes the stories explore? How do these themes relate to you?

Although some stories are new, many have also been around for a long time and are part of our classical heritage. However, whether contemporary or classical, all the stories have been chosen for their appeal to college students of all ages and from all walks of life. Happy reading!

Children
and
Adults

❖

Innocence
and
Experience

A Mother in Mannville

❖

Marjorie Rawlings

About the Author

Marjorie Rawlings was an American novelist and short story writer who spent most of her adult life in Florida. Her best-known novel, *The Yearling,* was awarded a Pulitzer Prize and made into a popular movie in 1946, starring Gregory Peck and Jane Wyman. Marjorie Rawlings died in 1953.

Something to Think About

How does our imagination help us cope with reality? What is perhaps an orphan's greatest wish?

Words to Keep in Mind

(The numbers in parentheses refer to the paragraphs in which the words first appear.)

rhododendron *(3)* shrub with pink, white, or purple flowers

hemlocks *(3)* poisonous plant with small white flowers

malaria *(5)* (literally, "bad air") disease transmitted by mosquitoes

corn shocks *(5)* stalks of corn stacked together to dry

mangled *(12)* mutilated, crippled

stoop *(14)* porch or step in front of a house

asters *(14)* plant with purplish flowers that bloom in fall

suffused *(20)* spread throughout

kindling *(23)* small pieces of dry wood used to start a fire

subterfuge *(28)* plan to hide the truth

treacherously *(32)* dangerously

impelled *(45)* driven

parturition *(49)* childbirth

thistledown *(71)* white, fluffy down formed on thistle, a weed with prickly leaves and stems and purple flowers

trifle *(73)* a little

abstracted *(73)* absent-minded

anomalous *(73)* abnormal

ecstasy *(74)* extreme happiness

vermilion *(74)* bright red

The orphanage is high in the Carolina mountains. Sometimes in   1
winter the snowdrifts are so deep that the institution is cut off from
the village below, from all the world. Fog hides the mountain peaks,
the snow swirls down the valleys, and a wind blows so bitterly that
the orphanage boys who take the milk twice daily to the baby cottage
reach the door with fingers stiff in an agony of numbness.

"Or when we carry trays from the cookhouse for the ones that are   2
sick," Jerry said, "we get our faces frostbit, because we can't put our
hands over them. I have gloves," he added. "Some of the boys don't
have any."

He liked the late spring, he said. The rhododendron was in bloom,   3
a carpet of color, across the mountainsides, soft as the May winds that
stirred the hemlocks. He called it laurel.

Reprinted with the permission of Scribner, a division of Simon & Schuster, from *When the Whippoorwill* by Marjorie Kinnan Rawlings. © 1936, 1940 by Marjorie Kinnan Rawlings; © renewed 1964, 1968 by Norton Baskin.

"It's pretty when the laurel blooms," he said. "Some of it's pink   4
and some of it's white."

I was there in the autumn. I wanted quiet, isolation, to do some   5
troublesome writing. I wanted mountain air to blow out the malaria
from too long a time in the subtropics. I was homesick, too, for the
flaming of maples in October, and for corn shocks and pumpkins and
black-walnut trees and the lift of hills. I found them all, living in a
cabin that belonged to the orphanage, half a mile beyond the orphanage
farm. When I took the cabin, I asked for a boy or man to come and chop
wood for the fireplace. The first few days were warm, I found what
wood I needed about the cabin, no one came, and I forgot the order.

I looked up from my typewriter one late afternoon, a little star-   6
tled. A boy stood at the door, and my pointer dog, my companion, was
at his side and had not barked to warn me. The boy was probably
twelve years old, but undersized. He wore overalls and a torn shirt,
and was barefooted.

He said, "I can chop some wood today."   7

I said, "But I have a boy coming from the orphanage."   8

"I'm the boy."   9

"You? But you're small."   10

"Size don't matter, chopping wood," he said. "Some of the big   11
boys don't chop good. I've been chopping wood at the orphanage a
long time."

I visualized mangled and inadequate branches for my fires. I was   12
well into my work and not inclined to conversation. I was a little
blunt.

"Very well. There's the ax. Go ahead and see what you can do."   13

I went back to work, closing the door. At first the sound of the   14
boy dragging brush annoyed me. Then he began to chop. The blows
were rhythmic and steady, and shortly I had forgotten him, the sound
no more of an interruption than a consistent rain. I suppose an hour
and a half passed, for when I stopped and stretched, and heard the
boy's steps on the cabin stoop, the sun was dropping behind the far-
thest mountain, and the valleys were purple with something deeper
than the asters.

The boy said, "I have to go to supper now. I can come again   15
tomorrow evening."

I said, "I'll pay you now for what you've done," thinking I should   16
probably have to insist on an older boy. "Ten cents an hour?"

"Anything is all right."   17

We went together back of the cabin. An astonishing amount of   18
solid wood had been cut. There were cherry logs and heavy roots of
rhododendron, and blocks from the waste pine and oak left from the
building of the cabin.

"But you've done as much as a man," I said, "This is a splendid   19
pile."

I looked at him, actually, for the first time. His hair was the color   20
of the corn shocks and his eyes, very direct, were like the mountain
sky when rain is pending—gray, with a shadowing of that miraculous
blue. As I spoke, a light came over him, as though the setting sun had
touched him with the same suffused glory with which it touched the
mountains. I gave him a quarter.

"You may come tomorrow," I said, "and thank you very much."   21

He looked at me, and at the coin, and seemed to want to speak,   22
but could not, and turned away.

"I'll split kindling tomorrow," he said over his thin ragged shoul-   23
der. "You'll need kindling and medium wood and logs and backlogs."

At daylight I was half wakened by the sound of chopping. Again it   24
was so even in texture that I went back to sleep. When I left my bed in
the cool morning, the boy had come and gone, and a stack of kindling
was neat against the cabin wall. He came again after school in the
afternoon and worked until time to return to the orphanage. His name
was Jerry; he was twelve years old, and he had been at the orphanage
since he was four. I could picture him at four, with the same grave
gray-blue eyes and the same—independence? No, the word that
comes to me is "integrity."

The word means something very special to me, and the quality for   25
which I use it is a rare one. My father had it—there is another of
whom I am almost sure—but almost no man of my acquaintance possesses it with the clarity, the purity, the simplicity of a mountain
stream. But the boy Jerry had it. It is bedded on courage, but it is
more than brave. It is honest, but it is more than honesty. The ax handle broke one day. Jerry said the woodshop at the orphanage would
repair it. I brought money to pay for the job and he refused it.

"I'll pay for it," he said. "I broke it. I brought the ax down care- 26
less."

"But no one hits accurately every time," I told him. "The fault 27
was in the wood of the handle. I'll see the man from whom I bought
it."

It was only then that he would take the money. He was standing 28
back of his own carelessness. He was a free-will agent and he chose
to do careful work, and if he failed, he took the responsibility without
subterfuge.

And he did for me the unnecessary thing, the gracious thing, that 29
we find done only by the great of heart. Things no training can teach,
for they are done on the instant, with no predicated experience. He
found a cubbyhole beside the fireplace that I had not noticed. There,
of his own accord, he put kindling and "medium" wood, so that I
might always have dry fire material ready in case of sudden wet
weather. A stone was loose in the rough walk to the cabin. He dug a
deeper hole and steadied it, although he came, himself, by a short cut
over the bank. I found that when I tried to return his thoughtfulness
with such things as candy and apples, he was wordless. "Thank you"
was, perhaps, an expression for which he had had no use, for his
courtesy was instinctive. He only looked at the gift and at me, and a
curtain lifted, so that I saw deep into the clear well of his eyes, and
gratitude was there, and affection, soft over the firm granite of his
character.

He made simple excuses to come and sit with me. I could no more 30
have turned him away than if he had been physically hungry. I suggested once that the best time for us to visit was just before supper,
when I left off my writing. After that, he waited always until my typewriter had been some time quiet. One day I worked until nearly dark.
I went outside the cabin, having forgotten him. I saw him going up
over the hill in the twilight toward the orphanage. When I sat down on
my stoop, a place was warm from his body where he had been sitting.

He became intimate, of course, with my pointer, Pat. There is a 31
strange communion between a boy and a dog. Perhaps they possess
the same singleness of spirit, the same kind of wisdom. It is difficult
to explain, but it exists. When I went across the state for a weekend, I
left the dog in Jerry's charge. I gave him the dog whistle and the key

to the cabin, and left sufficient food. He was to come two or three times a day and let out the dog, and feed and exercise him. I should return Sunday night, and Jerry would take out the dog for the last time Sunday afternoon and then leave the key under an agreed hiding place.

My return was belated and fog filled the mountain passes so   32 treacherously that I dared not drive at night. The fog held the next morning, and it was Monday noon before I reached the cabin. The dog had been fed and cared for that morning. Jerry came early in the afternoon, anxious.

"The superintendent said nobody would drive in the fog," he said.   33 "I came just before bedtime last night and you hadn't come. So I brought Pat some of my breakfast this morning. I wouldn't have let anything happen to him."

"I was sure of that. I didn't worry."   34

"When I heard about the fog, I thought you'd know."   35

He was needed for work at the orphanage and he had to return at   36 once. I gave him a dollar in payment, and he looked at it and went away. But that night he came in the darkness and knocked at the door.

"Come in, Jerry," I said, "if you're allowed to be away this late."   37

"I told maybe a story," he said. "I told them I thought you would   38 want to see me."

"That's true," I assured him, and I saw his relief. "I want to hear   39 about how you managed with the dog."

He sat by the fire with me, with no other light, and told me of   40 their two days together. The dog lay close to him, and found a comfort there that I did not have for him. And it seemed to me that being with my dog, and caring for him, had brought the boy and me, too, together, so that he felt that he belonged to me as well as to the animal.

"He stayed right with me," he told me, "except when he ran in the   41 laurel. He likes the laurel. I took him up over the hill and we both ran fast. There was a place where the grass was high and I lay down in it and hid. I could hear Pat hunting for me. He found my trail and he barked. When he found me, he acted crazy, and he ran around and around me, in circles."

We watched the flames.   42

"That's an apple log," he said. "It burns the prettiest of any 43
wood."

We were very close. 44

He was suddenly impelled to speak of things he had not spoken of 45
before, nor had I cared to ask him.

"You look a little bit like my mother," he said. "Especially in the 46
dark, by the fire."

"But you were only four, Jerry, when you came here. You have 47
remembered how she looked, all these years?"

"My mother lives in Mannville," he said. 48

For a moment, finding that he had a mother shocked me as 49
greatly as anything in my life has ever done, and I did not know
why it disturbed me. Then I understood my distress. I was filled
with a passionate resentment that any woman should go away and
leave her son. A fresh anger added itself. A son like this one—The
orphanage was a wholesome place, the executives were kind, good
people, the food was more than adequate, the boys were healthy, a
ragged shirt was no hardship, nor the doing of clean labor. Granted,
perhaps, that the boy felt no lack, what blood fed the bowels of a
woman who did not yearn over this child's lean body that had
come in parturition out of her own? At four he would have looked
the same as now. Nothing, I thought, nothing in life could change
those eyes. His quality must be apparent to an idiot, a fool. I burned
with questions I could not ask. In any case, I was afraid, there would
be pain.

"Have you seen her, Jerry—lately?" 50

"I see her every summer. She sends for me." 51

I wanted to cry out, "Why are you not with her? How can she let 52
you go away again?"

He said, "She comes up here from Mannville whenever she can. 53
She doesn't have a job now."

His face shone in the firelight. 54

"She wanted to give me a puppy, but they can't let any one boy 55
keep a puppy. You remember the suit I had on last Sunday?" He was
plainly proud. "She sent me that for Christmas. The Christmas before
that"—he drew a long breath, savoring the memory—"she sent me a
pair of skates."

"Roller skates?"   56

My mind was busy, making pictures of her, trying to understand   57
her. She had not, then, entirely deserted or forgotten him. But why,
then— I thought, "I must not condemn her without knowing."

"Roller skates. I let the other boys use them. They're always bor-   58
rowing them. But they're careful of them."

What circumstance other than poverty—   59

"I'm going to take the dollar you gave me for taking care of Pat,"   60
he said, "and buy her a pair of gloves."

I could only say, "That will be nice. Do you know her size?"   61

"I think it's 8½," he said.   62

He looked at my hands.   63

"Do you wear 8½?" he asked.   64

"No. I wear a smaller size, a 6."   65

"Oh! Then I guess her hands are bigger than yours."   66

I hated her. Poverty or no, there was other food than bread, and   67
the soul could starve as quickly as the body. He was taking his dollar
to buy gloves for her big stupid hands, and she lived away from him,
in Mannville, and contented herself with sending him skates.

"She likes white gloves," he said. "Do you think I can get them   68
for a dollar?"

"I think so," I said.   69

I decided that I should not leave the mountains without seeing her   70
and knowing for myself why she had done this thing.

The human mind scatters its interests as though made of thistle-   71
down, and every wind stirs and moves it. I finished my work. It did
not please me, and I gave my thoughts to another field. I should need
some Mexican material.

I made arrangements to close my Florida place. Mexico immedi-   72
ately, and doing the writing there, if conditions were favorable. Then,
Alaska with my brother. After that, heaven knew what or where.

I did not take time to go to Mannville to see Jerry's mother, nor   73
even to talk with the orphanage officials about her. I was a trifle
abstracted about the boy, because of my work and plans. And after my
first fury at her—we did not speak of her again—his having a mother,
any sort at all, not far away, in Mannville, relieved me of the ache I

had had about him. He did not question the anomalous relation. He was not lonely. It was none of my concern.

He came every day and cut my wood and did small helpful favors 74 and stayed to talk. The days had become cold, and often I let him come inside the cabin. He would lie on the floor in front of the fire, with one arm across the pointer, and they would both doze and wait quietly for me. Other days they ran with a common ecstasy through the laurel, and since the asters were now gone, he brought me back vermilion maple leaves, and chestnut boughs dripping with imperial yellow. I was ready to go.

I said to him, "You have been my good friend, Jerry. I shall often 75 think of you and miss you. Pat will miss you too. I am leaving tomorrow."

He did not answer. When he went away, I remember that a new 76 moon hung over the mountains, and I watched him go in silence up the hill. I expected him the next day, but he did not come. The details of packing my personal belongings, loading my car, arranging the bed over the seat, where the dog would ride, occupied me until late in the day. I closed the cabin and started the car, noticing that the sun was in the west and I should do well to be out of the mountains by nightfall. I stopped by the orphanage and left the cabin key and money for my light bill with Miss Clark.

"And will you call Jerry for me to say good-by to him?" 77

"I don't know where he is," she said. "I'm afraid he's not well. He 78 didn't eat his dinner this noon. One of the other boys saw him going over the hill into the laurel. He was supposed to fire the boiler this afternoon. It's not like him; he's unusually reliable."

I was almost relieved, for I knew I should never see him again, 79 and it would be easier not to say good-by to him.

I said, "I wanted to talk with you about his mother—why he's 80 here—but I'm in more of a hurry than I expected to be. It's out of the question for me to see her now too. But here's some money I'd like to leave with you to buy things for him at Christmas and on his birthday. It will be better than for me to try to send him things. I could so easily duplicate—skates, for instance."

She blinked her honest spinster's eyes. 81

"There's not much use for skates here," she said.   82

Her stupidity annoyed me.   83

"What I mean," I said, "is that I don't want to duplicate things his   84
mother sends him. I might have chosen skates if I didn't know she
had already given them to him."

She stared at me.   85

"I don't understand," she said. "He has no mother. He has no   86
skates."

Focusing on the Story

1. Why has the narrator come to the Carolina mountains? What is her
   occupation? What time of year is it? What do the mountains look
   like?
2. Who is Jerry and how does he meet the narrator?
3. The narrator says that Jerry has integrity. What does this term
   mean?
4. One day Jerry tells the narrator something that greatly shocks her.
   What does he tell her?
5. The narrator decides to go to Mannville to find out about Jerry's
   mother but then changes her mind. Why does she want to see the
   mother? Why does she change her mind?

Interpreting and Evaluating

1. At the beginning of the story, we learn that the narrator has contracted malaria in the subtropics and later that she'll close her place
   in Florida and travel to Mexico and Alaska. What can you infer
   from these comments about the narrator's lifestyle and economic
   status? What else can you say about the narrator?
2. When the narrator gives Jerry little gifts of candy and apples, Jerry
   is speechless. Why may he have trouble saying a simple "thank-
   you"?
3. Why does Jerry lie about his mother? Would you call Jerry a regular
   liar who should be punished? Explain.
4. Why does the narrator believe Jerry so readily? Does she really
   understand Jerry? How would you have reacted to Jerry's story?

5. How do you think the narrator feels after she has talked to Miss Clark at the orphanage at the end of the story? What does the narrator learn about people from this experience?

Ideas for Writing and Further Discussion

1. "A Mother in Mannville" contains some beautiful descriptive paragraphs. Reread the first page, and pay close attention to the descriptions. Then write two or three paragraphs describing a favorite place of your own at different times of the year. Start with a general sentence that expresses your feeling toward the place.

2. Does fantasy sometimes provide an important escape from a harsh reality? Write an essay about an incident in your life when your fantasy helped you cope. If you don't want to write about yourself, write about someone you know instead. What happened? How did the ability to dream or fantasize help you deal with the situation? It's not necessary to write a formal thesis statement in a narrative essay, but you may wish to start with a general statement that expresses an attitude toward the experience.

3. The author uses the anecdote about Jerry and the broken ax handle to illustrate the meaning of the word *integrity*. Choose an abstract word such as *courage, friendship,* or *maturity* that cannot be adequately defined by a simple word or phrase. Illustrate its meaning with an anecdote or a brief story. You may start by stating the dictionary definition of your word, and then tell the anecdote that illustrates what the word means to you.

4. The narrator admires Jerry for his many positive character traits. Even though he's only twelve, he appears instinctively courteous and gracious, sensitive to the needs of the narrator, independent, and mature. Write an essay in which you discuss some of his most admirable qualities and illustrate each quality with examples from the story.

   Suggested *thesis*: two or three qualities *or* two or three groups of similar qualities that the narrator admires in Jerry.

   Each *body paragraph* should illustrate one such quality (or group of related qualities) with details from the story.

5. Write an essay in which you compare and contrast the narrator and Jerry. Who is more sensitive to the needs of others? Are they both independent?

   Suggested *thesis*: two or three ways they are alike and/or different. Each *body paragraph* should explore one way they are alike or different.

Thank You M'am

❖

Langston Hughes

About the Author

Langston Hughes was an African-American writer who wrote books, poems, and short stories about everyday life in Harlem. He died in 1967.

 Something to Think About

What kind of a woman would you expect to have the name Mrs. Luella Bates Washington Jones? How would you expect such a woman to treat a boy who tries to steal her purse? How can kindness change a person's behavior?

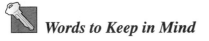 *Words to Keep in Mind*

sitter *(1)* slang for buttocks

frail *(16)* thin and delicate; weak

half nelson *(22)* wrestling term

S he was a large woman with a large purse that had everything in it   1
but a hammer and nails. It had a long strap, and she carried it slung
across her shoulder. It was about eleven o'clock at night, dark, and

From *Short Stories* by Langston Hughes. Reprinted by permission of Hill and Wang, a division of Farrar, Straus and Giroux, LLC. © 1996 by Ramona Bass and Arnold Rampersad.

she was walking alone, when a boy ran up behind her and tried to snatch her purse. The strap broke with the sudden single tug the boy gave it from behind. But the boy's weight and the weight of the purse combined caused him to lose his balance. Instead of taking off full blast as he had hoped, the boy fell on his back on the sidewalk and his legs flew up. The large woman simply turned around and kicked him right square in his blue-jeaned sitter. Then she reached down, picked the boy up by his shirt front, and shook him until his teeth rattled.

After that the woman said, "Pick up my pocketbook, boy, and give it here." 2

She still held him tightly. But she bent down enough to permit him to stoop and pick up her purse. Then she said, "Now ain't you ashamed of yourself?" 3

Firmly gripped by his shirt front, the boy said, "Yes'm." 4

The woman said, "What did you want to do it for?" 5

The boy said, "I didn't aim to." 6

She said, "You a lie!" 7

By that time two or three people passed, stopped, turned to look, and some stood watching. 8

"If I turn you loose, will you run?" asked the woman. 9

"Yes'm," said the boy. 10

"Then I won't turn you loose," said the woman. She did not release him. 11

"Lady, I'm sorry," whispered the boy. 12

"Um-hum! Your face is dirty. I got a great mind to wash your face for you. Ain't you got nobody home to tell you to wash your face?" 13

"No'm," said the boy. 14

"Then it will get washed this evening," said the large woman, starting up the street, dragging the frightened boy behind her. 15

He looked as if he were fourteen or fifteen, frail and willow-wild, in tennis shoes and blue jeans. 16

The woman said, "You ought to be my son. I would teach you right from wrong. Least I can do right now is to wash your face. Are you hungry?" 17

"No'm," said the being-dragged boy. "I just want you to turn me loose." 18

"Was I bothering *you* when I turned that corner?" asked the 19
woman.

"No'm." 20

"But you put yourself in contact with *me,*" said the woman. "If 21
you think that that contact is not going to last a while, you got another
thought coming. When I get through with you, sir, you are going to
remember Mrs. Luella Bates Washington Jones."

Sweat popped out on the boy's face and he began to struggle. 22
Mrs. Jones stopped, jerked him around in front of her, put a half nelson about his neck, and continued to drag him up the street. When she
got to her door, she dragged the boy inside, down a hall, and into a
large kitchenette-furnished room at the rear of the house. She
switched on the light and left the door open. The boy could hear other
roomers laughing and talking in the large house. Some of their doors
were open, too, so he knew he and the woman were not alone. The
woman still had him by the neck in the middle of her room.

She said, "What is your name?" 23

"Roger," answered the boy. 24

"Then, Roger, you go to that sink and wash your face," said the 25
woman, whereupon she turned him loose—at last. Roger looked at
the door—looked at the woman—looked at the door—*and went to the
sink.*

"Let the water run until it gets warm," she said. "Here's a clean 26
towel."

"You gonna take me to jail?" asked the boy, bending over the 27
sink.

"Not with that face, I would not take you nowhere," said the 28
woman. "Here I am trying to get home to cook me a bite to eat, and
you snatch my pocketbook! Maybe you ain't been to your supper
either, late as it be. Have you?"

"There's nobody home at my house," said the boy. 29

"Then we'll eat," said the woman. "I believe you're hungry—or 30
been hungry—to try to snatch my pocketbook!"

"I want a pair of blue suede shoes," said the boy. 31

"Well, you didn't have to snatch *my* pocketbook to get some 32
suede shoes," said Mrs. Luella Bates Washington Jones. "You could
of asked me."

"M'am?"   33

The water dripping from his face, the boy looked at her. There   34
was a long pause. A very long pause. After he had dried his face, and
not knowing what else to do, dried it again, the boy turned around,
wondering what next. The door was open. He could make a dash for it
down the hall. He could run, run, run, *run!*

The woman was sitting on the daybed. After a while she said, "I   35
were young once and I wanted things I could not get."

There was another long pause. The boy's mouth opened. Then he   36
frowned, not knowing he frowned.

The woman said, "Um-hum! You thought I was going to say *but,*   37
didn't you? You thought I was going to say, *but I didn't snatch people's pocketbooks.* Well, I wasn't going to say that." Pause. Silence. "I
have done things, too, which I would not tell you, son—neither tell
God, if He didn't already know. Everybody's got something in common. So you set down while I fix us something to eat. You might run
that comb through your hair so you will look presentable."

In another corner of the room behind a screen was a gas plate and   38
an icebox. Mrs. Jones got up and went behind the screen. The woman
did not watch the boy to see if he was going to run now, nor did she
watch her purse, which she left behind her on the daybed. But the boy
took care to sit on the far side of the room, away from the purse,
where be thought she could easily see him out of the corner of her eye
if she wanted to. He did not trust the woman *not* to trust him. And he
did not want to be mistrusted now.

"Do you need somebody to go to the store," asked the boy,   39
"maybe to get some milk or something?"

"Don't believe I do," said the woman, "unless you just want   40
sweet milk yourself. I was going to make cocoa out of this canned
milk I got here."

"That will be fine," said the boy.   41

She heated some lima beans and ham she had in the icebox, made   42
the cocoa, and set the table. The woman did not ask the boy anything
about where he lived, or his folks, or anything else that would embar-
rass him. Instead, as they ate, she told him about her job in a hotel
beauty shop that stayed open late, what the work was like, and how

all kinds of women came in and out, blondes, redheads, and Spanish. Then she cut him a half of her ten-cent cake.

"Eat some more, son," she said.   43

When they were finished eating, she got up and said, "Now here, 44 take this ten dollars and buy yourself some blue suede shoes. And next time, do not make the mistake of latching onto my pocketbook *nor nobody else's*—because shoes got by devilish ways will burn your feet. I got to get my rest now. But from here on in, son, I hope you will behave yourself."

She led him down the hall to the front door and opened it. "Good 45 night! Behave yourself, boy!" she said, looking out into the street as he went down the steps.

The boy wanted to say something other than, "Thank you, m'am," 46 to Mrs. Luella Bates Washington Jones, but although his lips moved, he couldn't even say that as he turned at the foot of the barren stoop and looked up at the large woman in the door. Then she shut the door.

Focusing on the Story

1. Describe the two characters in the story, Mrs. Luella Bates Washington Jones and Roger. Why are they both out on the street at eleven o'clock at night?
2. Why doesn't Roger run away after he tries to snatch Mrs. Jones's purse?
3. Describe Mrs. Jones's apartment. Does she have a lot of money?
4. What does Roger need money for?

Interpreting and Evaluating

1. Although Roger has tried to steal her purse, Mrs. Jones drags the boy home with her. Why doesn't she call the police?
2. Why doesn't Roger run away when Mrs. Jones finally turns him loose in the apartment? Why doesn't he "want to be mistrusted now"?
3. What kind of family life does Roger appear to have? Point to evidence in the story to support your view. Why can't he ask his parents for money?

4. Mrs. Jones says that she was "young once and . . . wanted things [she] couldn't get" and that she had "done things, too, that she couldn't tell." What may her childhood have been like? How may Mrs. Jones's childhood have been similar to Roger's?

5. Does Mrs. Jones do the right thing by rewarding Roger? Should Roger have been punished?

6. Why does Roger have trouble saying "thank you" at the end of the story? Do you think he has had much occasion to use this phrase? Explain.

7. Mrs. Jones says that Roger is "going to remember Mrs. Luella Bates Washington Jones." Why will Roger probably remember her? How do you think this episode will affect Roger's life and criminal activities?

Ideas for Writing and Further Discussion

1. Most of us would probably agree that we need more people like Mrs. Luella Bates Washington Jones. What are some of Mrs. Jones's personality traits that cause her to have an impact on Roger? Write an essay in which you discuss two or three of Mrs. Jones's positive traits (or two or three groups of similar traits), and show how and why these traits have an impact on Roger.
   Suggested *thesis*: two or three of Mrs. Jones's positive traits (or two or three groups of related traits).
   Each *body paragraph* should discuss one trait or group of related traits.

2. What are some causes of crime? Write an essay in which you discuss several major causes of crime as shown in the story.
   Suggested *thesis*: several causes of crime.
   Each *body paragraph* should explore one of the causes of crime.

3. Is incarceration—putting people in jail—the only way to reduce crime? Write an essay in which you discuss some ways to reduce crime.
   Suggested *thesis*: two or three ways to reduce crime.
   Each *body paragraph* should explore one way.

4. Can criminals be rehabilitated? Write an essay in which you discuss some ways to rehabilitate young criminal offenders.

Suggested *thesis*: two or three ways to rehabilitate young criminal offenders.

Each *body paragraph* should look at one such way.

Additional Ideas for Discussion and Writing

1. Although the woman (the writer who tells the story) in "A Mother in Mannville" by Marjorie Rawlings is educated, well-off, and white, she possesses little insight in basic human behavior. On the other hand, although Mrs. Luella Bates Washington Jones in "Thank You M'am" by Langston Hughes is uneducated, poor, and black, she is wise and knows quite a bit about human nature.

2. Write an essay in which you compare and contrast the writer in "A Mother in Mannville" and Mrs. Luella Bates Washington Jones in "Thank You M'am." Choose several areas or categories to compare and contrast, focusing on clear and striking contrasts such as education and life experience. Illustrate your points with examples from the two stories. In the conclusion, you may state which character is more perceptive and has the keenest wit.

   Suggested *thesis*: three or four categories to compare and/or contrast.

   Each *body paragraph* should explore one category or group of similar categories.

3. Compare and contrast Jerry, the orphan boy in "A Mother in Mannville" by Marjorie Rawlings and Mrs. Luella Bates Washington Jones in "Thank You M'am" by Langston Hughes. Focus on unexpected similarities. For example, even though Jerry is young, he is mature and wise, and, like Mrs. Luella Bates Washington Jones, has learned to cope with his situation in life. Overall then, like Mrs. Luella Bates Washington Jones, he may be able to impact others.

   Suggested *thesis*: several areas or categories to compare and contrast.

   Each *body paragraph* should explore one area or category and give examples from the stories to illustrate each point.

The Stolen Party

❖

Liliana Heker

About the Author

Liliana Heker, born in 1942, is an Argentine writer who published her first volume of short stories, *Those Who Beheld the Burning Bush,* while still in her teens. Later she became editor-in-chief of the literary magazine *El Ornitorrinco,* a forum for writers during the years of Argentina's brutal military dictatorships. Her novel, *Zona de Clivage,* won the Buenos Aires Municipal Prize.

Something to Think About

How do children and adults differ in their views of others? What do children admire in other children? On what do adults often base their views and attitudes toward others? What causes people to become more cynical and question the sincerity of those around them?

Words to Keep in Mind

pompously *(11)* proudly, self-importantly

charades *(38)* game of guessing a word by pantomiming or expressing the word or its syllables by gestures

As soon as she arrived she went straight to the kitchen to see if the 1 monkey was there. It was: what a relief! She wouldn't have liked to admit that her mother had been right. *Monkeys at a birthday?* her mother had sneered. *Get away with you, believing any nonsense you're told!* She was cross, but not because of the monkey, the girl thought; it's just because of the party.

"I don't like you going," she told her. "It's a rich people's party."   2

"Rich people go to Heaven too," said the girl, who studied reli-   3
gion at school.

"Get away with Heaven," said the mother. "The problem with   4
you, young lady, is that you like to fart higher than your ass."

The girl didn't approve of the way her mother spoke. She was   5
barely nine, and one of the best in her class.

"I'm going because I've been invited," she said. "And I've been   6
invited because Luciana is my friend. So there."

"Ah yes, your friend," her mother grumbled. She paused. "Listen,   7
Rosaura," she said at last. "That one's not your friend. You know
what you are to them? The maid's daughter, that's what."

Rosaura blinked hard: she wasn't going to cry. Then she yelled: 8
"Shut up! You know nothing about being friends!"

Every afternoon she used to go to Luciana's house and they   9
would both finish their homework while Rosaura's mother did the
cleaning. They had their tea in the kitchen and they told each other
secrets. Rosaura loved everything in the big house, and she also loved
the people who lived there.

"I'm going because it will be the most lovely party in the whole   10
world, Luciana told me it would. There will be a magician, and he
will bring a monkey and everything."

The mother swung around to take a good look at her child, and   11
pompously put her hands on her hips.

"Monkeys at a birthday?" she said. "Get away with you, believ-   12
ing any nonsense you're told!"

Rosaura was deeply offended. She thought it unfair of her mother   13
to accuse other people of being liars simply because they were rich.
Rosaura too wanted to be rich, of course. If one day she managed to
live in a beautiful palace, would her mother stop loving her? She felt

From *Other Fires:Short Fiction by Latin American Women* edited and translated by
Alberto Manguel. © 1982 by Liliana Heker. Translation © 1986 by Alberto Manguel.
Reprinted by permission of Crown Publishers, Inc., a division of Random House, Inc.
and Westwood Creative Artists, Ltd.

very sad. She wanted to go to that party more than anything else in the world.

"I'll die if I don't go," she whispered, almost without moving her 14
lips.

And she wasn't sure whether she had been heard, but on the 15
morning of the party she discovered that her mother had starched her
Christmas dress. And in the afternoon, after washing her hair, her
mother rinsed it in apple vinegar so that it would be all nice and shiny.
Before going out, Rosaura admired herself in the mirror, with her
white dress and glossy hair, and thought she looked terribly pretty.

Señora Ines also seemed to notice. As soon as she saw her, she said: 16
"How lovely you look today, Rosaura." 17

Rosaura gave her starched skirt a slight toss with her hands and 18
walked into the party with a firm step. She said hello to Luciana and
asked about the monkey. Luciana put on a secretive look and whispered into Rosaura's ear: "He's in the kitchen. But don't tell anyone,
because it's a surprise."

Rosaura wanted to make sure. Carefully she entered the kitchen 19
and there she saw it: deep in thought, inside its cage. It looked so
funny that the girl stood there for a while, watching it, and later, every
so often, she would slip out of the party unseen and go and admire it.
Rosaura was the only one allowed into the kitchen. Señora Ines had
said: "You yes, but not the others, they're much too boisterous, they
might break something." Rosaura had never broken anything. She
even managed the jug of orange juice, carrying it from the kitchen
into the dining room. She held it carefully and didn't spill a single
drop. And Señora Ines had said: "Are you sure you can manage a jug
as big as that?" Of course she could manage. She wasn't a butter-
fingers, like the others. Like that blonde girl with the bow in her hair.
As soon as she saw Rosaura, the girl with the bow had said:

"And you? Who are you?" 20

"I'm a friend of Luciana," said Rosaura. 21

"No," said the girl with the bow, "you are not a friend of Luciana 22
because I'm her cousin and I know all her friends. And I don't know
you."

"So what," said Rosaura. "I come here every afternoon with my 23
mother and we do our homework together."

"You and your mother do your homework together?" asked the   24
girl, laughing.

"I and Luciana do our homework together," said Rosaura, very   25
seriously.

The girl with the bow shrugged her shoulders.   26

"That's not being friends," she said. "Do you go to school   27
together?"

"No."   28

"So where do you know her from?" said the girl, getting impa-   29
tient.

Rosaura remembered her mother's words perfectly. She took a   30
deep breath.

"I'm the daughter of the employee," she said.   31

Her mother had said very clearly: "If someone asks, you say   32
you're the daughter of the employee; that's all." She also told her to
add: "And proud of it." But Rosaura thought that never in her life
would she dare say something of the sort.

"What employee?" said the girl with the bow. "Employee in a   33
shop?"

"No," said Rosaura angrily. "My mother doesn't sell anything in   34
any shop, so there."

"So how come she's an employee?" said the girl with the bow.   35

Just then Señora Ines arrived saying *shh shh,* and asked Rosaura   36
if she wouldn't mind helping serve out the hotdogs, as she knew the
house so much better than the others.

"See?" said Rosaura to the girl with the bow, and when no one   37
was looking she kicked her in the shin.

Apart from the girl with the bow, all the others were delightful.   38
The one she liked best was Luciana, with her golden birthday crown;
and then the boys. Rosaura won the sack race, and nobody managed
to catch her when they played tag. When they split into two teams to
play charades, all the boys wanted her for their side. Rosaura felt she
had never been so happy in all her life.

But the best was still to come. The best came after Luciana blew   39
out the candles. First the cake. Señora Ines had asked her to help pass
the cake around, and Rosaura had enjoyed the task immensely,
because everyone called out to her, shouting "Me, me!" Rosaura
remembered a story in which there was a queen who had the power of

life or death over her subjects. She had always loved that, having the power of life or death. To Luciana and the boys she gave the largest pieces, and to the girl with the bow she gave a slice so thin one could see through it.

After the cake came the magician, tall and bony, with a fine red 40 cape. A true magician: he could untie handkerchiefs by blowing on them and make a chain with links that had no openings. He could guess what cards were pulled out from a pack, and the monkey was his assistant. He called the monkey "partner." "Let's see here, partner," he would say, "turn over a card." And, "Don't run away, partner: time to work now."

The final trick was wonderful. One of the children had to hold the 41 monkey in his arms and the magician said he would make him disappear.

"What, the boy?" they all shouted. 42

"No, the monkey!" shouted back the magician. 43

Rosaura thought that this was truly the most amusing party in the 44 whole world.

The magician asked a small fat boy to come and help, but the 45 small fat boy got frightened almost at once and dropped the monkey on the floor. The magician picked him up carefully, whispered something in his ear, and the monkey nodded almost as if he understood.

"You mustn't be so unmanly, my friend," the magician said to the 46 fat boy.

"What's unmanly?" said the fat boy. 47

The magician turned around as if to look for spies. 48

"A sissy," said the magician. "Go sit down." 49

Then he stared at all the faces, one by one. Rosaura felt her heart 50 tremble.

"You, with the Spanish eyes," said the magician. And everyone 51 saw that he was pointing at her.

She wasn't afraid. Neither holding the monkey, nor when the 52 magician made him vanish; not even when, at the end, the magician flung his red cape over Rosaura's head and uttered a few magic words . . . and the monkey reappeared, chattering happily, in her arms. The children clapped furiously. And before Rosaura returned to her seat, the magician said:

"Thank you very much, my little countess." 53

She was so pleased with the compliment that a while later, when   54
her mother came to fetch her, that was the first thing she told her.

"I helped the magician and he said to me, 'Thank you very much,   55
my little countess.'"

It was strange because up to then Rosaura had thought that she was   56
angry with her mother. All along Rosaura had imagined that she would
say to her: "See that the monkey wasn't a lie?" But instead she was so
thrilled that she told her mother all about the wonderful magician.

Her mother tapped her on the head and said: "So now we're a   57
countess!"

But one could see that she was beaming.   58

And now they both stood in the entrance, because a moment ago   59
Señora Ines, smiling, had said: "Please wait here a second."

Her mother suddenly seemed worried.   60

"What is it?" she asked Rosaura.   61

"What is what?" said Rosaura. "It's nothing; she just wants to get   62
the presents for those who are leaving, see?"

She pointed at the fat boy and at a girl with pigtails who were also   63
waiting there, next to their mothers. And she explained about the
presents. She knew, because she had been watching those who left
before her. When one of the girls was about to leave, Señora Ines
would give her a bracelet. When a boy left, Señora Ines gave him a
yo-yo. Rosaura preferred the yo-yo because it sparkled, but she didn't
mention that to her mother. Her mother might have said: "So why
don't you ask for one, you blockhead?" That's what her mother was
like. Rosaura didn't feel like explaining that she'd be horribly
ashamed to be the odd one out. Instead she said:

"I was the best-behaved at the party."   64

And she said no more because Señora Ines came out into the hall   65
with two bags, one pink and one blue.

First she went up to the fat boy, gave him a yo-yo out of the blue   66
bag, and the fat boy left with his mother. Then she went up to the girl
and gave her a bracelet out of the pink bag, and the girl with the pigtails left as well.

Finally she came up to Rosaura and her mother. She had a big   67
smile on her face and Rosaura liked that. Señora Ines looked down at
her, then looked up at her mother, and then said something that made
Rosaura proud:

"What a marvelous daughter you have, Herminia."   68

For an instant, Rosaura thought that she'd give her two presents: 69
the bracelet and the yo-yo. Señora Ines bent down as if about to look
for something. Rosaura also leaned forward, stretching out her arm.
But she never completed the movement.

Señora Ines didn't look in the pink bag. Nor did she look in the blue   70
bag. Instead she rummaged in her purse. In her hand appeared two bills.

"You really and truly earned this," she said handing them over.   71
"Thank you for all your help, my pet."

Rosaura felt her arms stiffen, stick close to her body, and then she   72
noticed her mother's hand on her shoulder. Instinctively she pressed herself against her mother's body. That was all. Except her eyes. Rosaura's
eyes had a cold, clear look that fixed itself on Señora Ines's face.

Señora Ines, motionless, stood there with her hand outstretched.   73
As if she didn't dare draw it back. As if the slightest change might
shatter an infinitely delicate balance.

Focusing on the Story

1. Describe Rosaura. How does her attitude differ from that of her
   mother? How and why is this difference established at the beginning of the story?
2. Why doesn't the mother want Rosaura to go to the birthday party?
   Doesn't she want her daughter to be happy?
3. Do Rosaura and Luciana attend the same school? Why do they do
   their homework together?
4. How does Rosaura feel about herself? Does she like helping Señora
   Ines serve orange juice, hotdogs, and cake? How does she get along
   with the other children at the party?
5. What do the other children receive when they leave the party? What
   does Rosaura get? Why does Señora Ines distinguish between
   Rosaura and the other children?

Interpreting and Evaluating

1. What does the title "The Stolen Party" refer to? Who "stole" the
   party and in what ways?

2. How do you think Rosaura's home life differs from Luciana's? How would a birthday party in Rosaura's neighborhood differ from Luciana's party?
3. When Señora Ines hands Rosaura the money, Rosaura feels "her arms stiffen." Why doesn't Rosaura like being paid for helping Señora Ines? How would you have felt if you had been in Rosaura's place?
4. At the end of the story, Señora Ines "stood there with her hand out-stretched . . . as if the slightest change might shatter an infinitely delicate balance." What is this "delicate balance"?
5. What do you think Rosaura's prospects are in life? To what extent will her social class limit her options? Do you think Luciana will continue to invite Rosaura to her house when she reaches high school and college? Why or why not? What comment does the story make on the division of social classes in Argentina?

Ideas for Writing and Further Discussion

1. At the beginning of the story, the author focuses on the conflict between Rosaura and her mother. What's another more important conflict in the short story? In two or three paragraphs, explore the two conflicts in the story. Which one is resolved?
2. At the end of the story, Rosaura has lost some of her innocence or naïveté. Like her mother, she'll probably become more skeptical and less likely to believe in the goodness of others. Think of an incident when you became more cynical and discovered the phoniness in others. Write about a time when such a change occurred in you. Describe what happened. What did somebody say or do? How did it affect you, and why do you think it affected you that way? It's not necessary to write a formal thesis statement in a narrative essay, but you may wish to start with a general statement that expresses your attitude toward the experience.
3. In a few paragraphs, describe your relationship with your mother and compare it to either or both of the mother-daughter pairs in the story. Do you feel that your mother, like Rosaura's mother, keeps reminding you of your limitations such as age, intelligence, and background, or does she encourage you to break such boundaries?

The Open Window

❖

Saki

About the Author

Born in Burma, Saki, whose real name was Hector Hugh Munro, was a Scottish novelist and short story writer who took the name Saki from an old Persian poem. His inventive and imaginative stories often satirize British society.

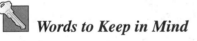

Something to Think About

Have you ever played a prank on somebody? When is a prank no longer a prank?

Words to Keep in Mind

endeavored *(2)* tried

rectory *(5)* the house in which a minister or priest lives

moor *(13)* open wasteland, often wet and covered with heather (British)

snipe *(13)* long-billed wading bird that lives in marshy places

bog *(13)* a small marsh

engulfed *(13)* swallowed up; absorbed completely

treacherous *(13)* dangerous; not to be trusted

marshes *(17)* low, soft lands, temporarily or permanently covered with water

delusion *(18)* a false opinion sometimes resulting from mental illness

ailments *(18)* illnesses

infirmities *(18)* weaknesses

imminent *(23)* likely to happen right away

Ganges *(26)* river in North India and Bangladesh

pariah dogs *(26)* wild, despised animals

My aunt will be down presently, Mr. Nuttel," said a very self-possessed young lady of fifteen; "in the meantime you must try and put up with me." 1

Framton Nuttel endeavored to say the correct something which should duly flatter the niece of the moment without unduly discounting the aunt that was to come. Privately he doubted more than ever whether these formal visits on a succession of total strangers would do much towards helping the nerve cure which he was supposed to be undergoing. 2

"I know how it will be," his sister had said when he was preparing to migrate to this rural retreat; "you will bury yourself down there and not speak to a living soul, and your nerves will be worse than ever from moping. I shall just give you letters of introduction to all the people I know there. Some of them, as far as I can remember, were quite nice." Framton wondered whether Mrs. Sappleton, the lady to whom he was presenting one of the letters of introduction, came into the nice division. 3

"Do you know many of the people round here?" asked the niece, when she judged that they had had sufficient silent communion. 4

"Hardly a soul," said Framton. "My sister was staying here, at the rectory, you know, some four years ago, and she gave me letters of introduction to some of the people here." 5

He made the last statement in a tone of distinct regret. 6

"Then you know practically nothing about my aunt?" pursued the self-possessed young lady. 7

From *The Short Stories of Saki* (H. H. Munro). © 1930 by The Viking Press, Inc.

"Only her name and address," admitted the caller. He was won- 8
dering whether Mrs. Sappleton was in the married or widowed state.
An undefinable something about the room seemed to suggest masculine habitation.

"Her great tragedy happened just three years ago," said the child; 9
"that would be since your sister's time."

"Her tragedy?" asked Framton; somehow in this restful country 10
spot tragedies seemed out of place.

"You may wonder why we keep that window wide open on an 11
October afternoon," said the niece, indicating a large French window
that opened onto a lawn.

"It is quite warm for the time of the year," said Framton; "but has 12
that window got anything to do with the tragedy?"

"Out through that window, three years ago to a day, her husband 13
and her two young brothers went off for their day's shooting. They
never came back. In crossing the moor to their favorite snipe-shooting
ground they were all three engulfed in a treacherous piece of bog. It
had been that dreadful wet summer, you know, and places that were
safe in other years gave way suddenly without warning. Their bodies
were never recovered. That was the dreadful part of it." Here the
child's voice lost its self-possessed note and became falteringly
human. "Poor aunt always thinks that they will come back some day,
they and the little brown spaniel that was lost with them, and walk in
at that window just as they used to do. That is why the window is kept
open every evening till it is quite dusk. Poor dear aunt, she has often
told me how they went out, her husband with his white waterproof
coat over his arm, and Ronnie, her youngest brother, singing, 'Bertie,
why do you bound?' as he always did to tease her, because she said it
got on her nerves. Do you know, sometimes on still, quiet evenings
like this, I almost get a creepy feeling that they will all walk in
through that window—"

She broke off with a little shudder. It was a relief to Framton 14
when the aunt bustled into the room with a whirl of apologies for
being late in making her appearance.

"I hope Vera has been amusing you?" she said. 15

"She has been very interesting," said Framton. 16

"I hope you don't mind the open window," said Mrs. Sappleton   17
briskly; "my husband and brothers will be home directly from shooting, and they always come in this way. They've been out for snipe in
the marshes today, so they'll make a fine mess over my poor carpets.
So like you menfolk, isn't it?" She rattled on cheerfully about the
shooting and the scarcity of birds, and the prospects for duck in the
winter. To Framton it was all purely horrible. He made a desperate
effort to turn the talk onto a less ghastly topic; he was conscious that
his hostess was giving him only a fragment of her attention, and her
eyes were constantly straying past him to the open window and the
lawn beyond. It was certainly an unfortunate coincidence that he
should have paid his visit on this tragic anniversary.

"The doctors agree in ordering me complete rest, an absence of   18
mental excitement, and avoidance of any violent physical exercise,"
announced Framton, who labored under the tolerably widespread
delusion that total strangers and chance acquaintances are hungry for
the least detail of one's ailments and infirmities. "On the matter of
diet they are not so much in agreement," he continued.

"No?" said Mrs. Sappleton, in a voice which only replaced a   19
yawn at the last moment. Then she suddenly brightened into alert
attention—but not to what Framton was saying.

"Here they are at last!" she cried. "Just in time for tea, and don't   20
they look as if they were muddy up to the eyes!"

Framton shivered slightly and turned towards the niece with a   21
look intended to convey sympathetic comprehension. The child was
staring out through the open window with dazed horror in her eyes. In
a chill shock of nameless fear Framton swung round in his seat and
looked in the same direction.

In the deepening twilight three figures were walking across the   22
lawn towards the window; they all carried guns under their arms, and
one of them was additionally burdened with a white coat hung over
his shoulders. A tired brown spaniel kept close at their heels.
Noiselessly they neared the house, and then a hoarse young voice
chanted out of the dusk: "I said, Bertie, why do you bound?"

Framton grabbed wildly at his stick and hat; the hall door, the   23
gravel drive, and the front gate were dimly noted stages in his head-

long retreat. A cyclist coming along the road had to run into the hedge to avoid imminent collision.

"Here we are, my dear," said the bearer of the white mackintosh, 24 coming in through the window; "fairly muddy, but most of it's dry. Who was that who bolted out as we came up?"

"A most extraordinary man, a Mr. Nuttel," said Mrs. Sappleton; 25 "could only talk about his illnesses, and dashed off without a word of good-by or apology when you arrived. One would think he had seen a ghost."

"I expect it was the spaniel," said the niece calmly; "he told me he 26 had a horror of dogs. He was once hunted into a cemetery somewhere on the banks of the Ganges by a pack of pariah dogs, and had to spend the night in a newly dug grave with the creatures snarling and grinning and foaming just above him. Enough to make anyone lose their nerve."

Romance at short notice was her speciality. 27

Focusing on the Story

1. Why has Framton Nuttel come to stay in the English countryside?
2. According to Vera, the niece, what was the tragedy that was supposed to have happened three years ago? Did it really happen?
3. Vera, Mrs. Sappleton's niece, is described as "a very self-possessed young lady of fifteen." What other words could be used to describe her?
4. Why does Framton Nuttel grab "wildly at his stick and hat" and bolt out the door? What does he think he has seen coming through the open window? Who is really coming through the window?
5. How does Vera, the niece, explain Mr. Nuttel's sudden departure?

Interpreting and Evaluating

1. How does the name Framton Nuttel reflect Mr. Nuttel's character?
2. In what ways is Framton Nuttel different from the niece?
3. Why does Vera tell Framton Nuttel such a bizarre story, and why does Framton believe it?

4. The author uses some very formal words and phrases such as *endeavor, sufficient silent communion,* and *masculine habitation,* in addition to some overly long sentences. What effect does such formal language have on the story? How does it contribute to the humor? What does Saki ridicule in this story?

5. The last sentence, "Romance at short notice was her speciality," refers to the niece. What does it mean? Could the statement also refer to the author? Explain.

Ideas for Writing and Further Discussion

1. Write about a time when you played a prank on someone. What did you do? Who was the butt of your joke? How do you think he or she felt? What would you have done if the prank had backfired?

2. Write about a time when someone played a prank on you. Who was your tormentor or prankster? What happened? How did it make you feel? It's not necessary to write a formal thesis statement in a narrative essay, but you may wish to start with a general sentence that introduces the event and expresses your attitude toward the incident.

The Little Match Girl

❖

Hans Christian Andersen

About the Author

Hans Christian Andersen was the son of a poor shoemaker and grew up in a small town in Denmark in the 1800s. At that time, the Scandinavian countries were among the poorest in Europe. Andersen's stories, whose characters are mostly poor, were read by almost everyone, even the kings and queens. Soon people started to demand a change in the social system. Today the Scandinavian countries have the highest standard of living in the world. Other famous stories by Andersen include "The Emperor's New Clothes," "The Little Mermaid," and "The Ugly Duckling."

Something to Think About

Can dramatic fiction about social problems help correct social ills? Hans Christian Andersen's stories were read by the kings and queens in Scandinavia. What impact may the following story have had on them?

It was so terribly cold. Snow was falling, and it was almost dark. 1
Evening came on, the last evening of the year. In the cold and gloom a poor little girl, bareheaded and barefoot, was walking through the streets. Of course when she had left her house she'd had slippers on, but what good had they been? They were very big slippers, way too big for her, for they belonged to her mother. The little girl had lost them running across the road, where two carriages had rattled by

terribly fast. One slipper she'd not been able to find again, and a boy had run off with the other, saying he could use it very well as a cradle some day when he had children of his own. And so the little girl walked on her naked feet, which were quite red and blue with the cold. In an old apron she carried several packages of matches, and she held a box of them in her hand. No one had bought any from her all day long, and no one had given her a cent.

Shivering with cold and hunger, she crept along, a picture of misery, poor little girl! The snowflakes fell on her long fair hair, which hung in pretty curls over her neck. But she didn't think of her pretty curls now. In all the windows lights were shining, and there was a wonderful smell of roast goose, for it was New Year's Eve. Yes, she thought of that! 2

In a corner formed by two houses, one of which projected farther out into the street than the other, she sat down and drew up her little feet under her. She was getting colder and colder, but did not dare to go home, for she had sold no matches, nor earned a single cent, and her father would surely beat her. Besides, it was cold at home, for they had nothing over them but a roof through which the wind whistled even though the biggest cracks had been stuffed with straw and rags. 3

Her hands were almost dead with cold. Oh, how much one little match might warm her! If she could only take one from the box and rub it against the wall and warm her hands. She drew one out. *R-r-ratch!* How it sputtered and burned! It made a warm, bright flame, like a little candle, as she held her hands over it; but it gave a strange light! It really seemed to the little girl as if she were sitting before a great iron stove with shining brass knobs and a brass cover. How wonderfully the fire burned! How comfortable it was! The youngster stretched out her feet to warm them too; then the little flame went out, the stove vanished, and she had only the remains of the burnt match in her hand. 4

She struck another match against the wall. It burned brightly, and when the light fell upon the wall it became transparent like a thin veil, and she could see through it into a room. On the table a snow-white cloth was spread, and on it stood a shining dinner service. The roast goose steamed gloriously, stuffed with apples and prunes. And what was still better, the goose jumped down from the dish and waddled 5 along the floor, with a knife and fork in its breast, right over to the little girl. Then the match went out, and she could see only the thick, cold wall. She lighted another match. Then she was sitting under the most beautiful Christmas tree. It was much larger and much more beautiful than the one she had seen last Christmas through the glass door at the rich merchant's home. Thousands of candles burned on the green branches, and colored pictures like those in the printshops looked down at her. The little girl reached both her hands toward them. Then the match went out. But the Christmas lights mounted higher. She saw them now as bright stars in the sky. One of them fell down, forming a long line of fire.

"Now someone is dying," thought the little girl, for her old grandmother, the only person who had loved her, and who was now dead, had told her that when a star fell down a soul went up to God. 6

She rubbed another match against the wall. It became bright again, and in the glow the old grandmother stood clear and shining, kind and lovely. 7

"Grandmother!" cried the child. "Oh, take me with you! I know you will disappear when the match is burned out. You will vanish like the warm stove, the wonderful roast goose and the beautiful big Christmas tree!" 8

And she quickly struck the whole bundle of matches, for she wished to keep her grandmother with her. And the matches burned with such a glow that it became brighter than daylight. Grandmother had never been so grand and beautiful. She took the little girl in her arms, and both of them flew in brightness and joy above the earth, very, very high, and up there was neither cold, nor hunger, nor fear— they were with God. 9

But in the corner, leaning against the wall, sat the little girl with red cheeks and smiling mouth, frozen to death on the last evening of the old year. The New Year's sun rose upon a little pathetic figure. The child sat there, stiff and cold, holding the matches, of which one bundle was almost burned. 10

"She wanted to warm herself," the people said. No one imagined what beautiful things she had seen, and how happily she had gone with her old grandmother into the bright New Year. 11

Focusing on the Story

1. Describe the little girl as she's walking through the cold streets. About how old is she? What has happened to her shoes?
2. Describe the setting (time and place) of the story.
3. How does the little girl feel? Why is she unable to go home? Why does she burn all her matches, and what does she "see" in the burning flames?
4. What do people see the next morning, New Year's Day? What do they say when they see the burned matches?

Interpreting and Evaluating

1. What is the author's attitude toward the little girl? In other words, what is the story's tone? What words and phrases has the author chosen to convey this attitude or tone? Do you feel sympathy for the girl?
2. Describe your own feelings as you were reading the three last paragraphs of the story. What accounts for the strong emotional impact (the story's mood) of the ending?
3. How would you react if you came across the little girl, frozen to death, holding her burned matches?
4. Does anyone in our society today remind you of the little match girl? If so, who?
5. It has been said that the poor will always be with us. Do you agree with this statement? What can be done to prevent poverty?

Ideas for Writing and Further Discussion

Andersen writes that the little girl "did not dare to go home, for she had sold no matches, nor earned a single cent, and her father would surely beat her." Could such blatant child neglect or abuse occur in our society today? Are child abuse and poverty connected? Do you know of any place where child labor still exists?

1. Write an essay in which you explore reasons why child abuse occurs. Use examples from your own experience or from research to illustrate your points.

Suggested *thesis*: two or three reasons why child abuse occurs in certain families or areas.

Each *body paragraph* should explore one cause and give examples that illustrate how that one cause leads to child abuse.

2. Write an essay in which you discuss several steps that have been taken to prevent child labor and hunger in our own country.

Suggested *thesis*: two or three social programs that help alleviate each of these social ills.

Each *body paragraph* should explore one program and show how it alleviates social problems.

An Additional Idea for Discussion and Writing

Discuss or write an essay in which you compare and contrast Jerry, the orphan boy in "A Mother in Mannville" by Marjorie Rawlings, and the little girl in "The Little Match Girl" by Hans Christian Andersen. How are they similar? How do they differ? For example, do they both resort to illusion and fantasy to deal with their harsh realities? How do their illusions differ? What are the results of their dreams?

Suggested *thesis*: two or three areas (categories) that are similar or different.

Each *body paragraph* should explore one area or category and include examples from the stories to illustrate each point.

Charles

❖

Shirley Jackson

About the Author

Shirley Jackson was an American novelist and short story writer who grew up in California. Many of her works have been adapted for radio and television. Her most famous short story, "The Lottery," a contemporary horror story, appears in many anthologies. She has also written many novels, including *The Haunting of Hill House*. She died in 1965.

Something to Think About

It's often difficult to take responsibility for our own actions. Have you ever blamed somebody else for something you did?

Words to Keep in Mind

renounced *(1)* gave up

tot *(1)* small child

swaggering *(1)* arrogant, showing off

raucous *(2)* loud and rowdy

insolently *(3)* disrespectfully

pounding *(20)* banging or hitting hard

deprived *(20)* kept from having

scornfully *(33)* full of contempt

scanning *(63)* looking at closely in a searching way

matronly *(63)* like a mature woman

primly *(68)* stiffly formal

lapses *(68)* slips or falls

The day my son Laurie started kindergarten he renounced cor- 1
duroy overalls with bibs and began wearing blue jeans with a belt; I
watched him go off the first morning with the older girl next door,
seeing clearly that an era of my life was ended, my sweet-voiced
nursery-school tot replaced by a long-trousered, swaggering character
who forgot to stop at the corner and wave good-bye to me.

He came home the same way, the front door slamming open, his 2
cap on the floor, and the voice suddenly become raucous shouting,
"Isn't anybody *here*?"

At lunch he spoke insolently to his father, spilled his baby sister's 3
milk, and remarked that his teacher said we were not to take the name
of the Lord in vain.

"How *was* school today?" I asked, elaborately casual. 4

"All right," he said. 5

"Did you learn anything?" his father asked. 6

Laurie regarded his father coldly. "I didn't learn nothing," he 7
said.

"Anything," I said. "Didn't learn anything." 8

"The teacher spanked a boy, though," Laurie said, addressing his 9
bread and butter. "For being fresh," he added, with his mouth full.

"What did he do?" I asked. "Who was it?" 10

Laurie thought. "It was Charles," he said. "He was fresh. The 11
teacher spanked him and made him stand in a corner. He was awfully
fresh."

"What did he do?" I asked again, but Laurie slid off his chair, 12
took a cookie, and left, while his father was still saying, "See here,
young man."

The next day Laurie remarked at lunch, as soon as he sat down, 13 "Well, Charles was bad again today." He grinned enormously and said, "Today Charles hit the teacher."

"Good heavens," I said, mindful of the Lord's name, "I suppose 14 he got spanked again?"

"He sure did," Laurie said. "Look up," he said to his father.   15

"What?" his father said, looking up.   16

"Look down," Laurie said. "Look at my thumb. Gee, you're 17 dumb." He began to laugh insanely.

"Why did Charles hit the teacher?" I asked quickly.   18

"Because she tried to make him color with red crayons," Laurie 19 said. "Charles wanted to color with green crayons so he hit the teacher and she spanked him and said nobody play with Charles but everybody did."

The third day—it was Wednesday of the first week—Charles 20 bounced a see-saw onto the head of a little girl and made her bleed, and the teacher made him stay inside all during recess. Thursday Charles had to stand in a corner during story-time because he kept pounding his feet on the floor. Friday Charles was deprived of blackboard privileges because he threw chalk.

On Saturday I remarked to my husband, "Do you think kinder- 21 garten is too unsettling for Laurie? All this toughness, and bad grammar, and this Charles boy sounds like such a bad influence."

"It'll be all right," my husband said reassuringly. "Bound to be 22 people like Charles in the world. Might as well meet them now as later."

On Monday Laurie came home late, full of news. "Charles," he 23 shouted as he came up the hill; I was waiting anxiously on the front steps. "Charles," Laurie yelled all the way up the hill, "Charles was bad again."

"Come right in," I said, as soon as he came close enough. "Lunch 24 is waiting."

"You know what Charles did?" he demanded, following me 25 through the door. "Charles yelled so in school they sent a boy in from first grade to tell the teacher she had to make Charles keep quiet, and so Charles had to stay after school. And so all the children stayed to watch him."

"What did he do?" I asked.   26

"He just sat there," Laurie said, climbing into his chair at the   27
table. "Hi, Pop, y'old dust mop."

"Charles had to stay after school today," I told my husband.   28
"Everyone stayed with him."

"What does this Charles look like?" my husband asked Laurie.   29
"What's his other name?"

"He's bigger than me," Laurie said. "And he doesn't have any   30
rubbers and he doesn't ever wear a jacket."

Monday night was the first Parent-Teachers meeting, and only the   31
fact that the baby had a cold kept me from going; I wanted passion-
ately to meet Charles's mother. On Tuesday Laurie remarked suddenly, "Our teacher had a friend come to see her in school today."

"Charles's mother?" my husband and I asked simultaneously.   32

"Naaah," Laurie said scornfully. "It was a man who came and   33
made us do exercises, we had to touch our toes. Look." He climbed
down from his chair and squatted down and touched his toes. "Like
this," he said. He got solemnly back into his chair and said, picking
up his fork, "Charles didn't even *do* exercises."

"That's fine," I said heartily. "Didn't Charles want to do exer-   34
cises?"

"Naaah," Laurie said. "Charles was so fresh to the teacher's   35
friend he wasn't *let* do exercises."

"Fresh again?" I said.   36

"He kicked the teacher's friend," Laurie said. "The teacher's   37
friend told Charles to touch his toes like I just did and Charles kicked
him."

"What are they going to do about Charles, do you suppose?"   38
Laurie's father asked him.

Laurie shrugged elaborately. "Throw him out of school, I guess,"   39
he said.

Wednesday and Thursday were routine; Charles yelled during   40
story hour and hit a boy in the stomach and made him cry. On Friday
Charles stayed after school again and so did all the other children.

With the third week of kindergarten Charles was an institution in   41
our family; the baby was being a Charles when she cried all afternoon; Laurie did a Charles when he filled his wagon full of mud and
pulled it through the kitchen; even my husband, when he caught his

elbow in the telephone cord and pulled telephone, ashtray, and a bowl of flowers off the table, said, after the first minute, "Looks like Charles."

During the third and fourth weeks it looked like a reformation in 42 Charles; Laurie reported grimly at lunch on Thursday of the third week, "Charles was so good today the teacher gave him an apple."

"What?" I said, and my husband added warily, "You mean 43 Charles?"

"Charles," Laurie said. "He gave the crayons around and he 44 picked up the books afterward and the teacher said he was her helper."

"What happened?" I asked incredulously. 45

"He was her helper, that's all," Laurie said, and shrugged. 46

"Can this be true, about Charles?" I asked my husband that night. 47 "Can something like this happen?"

"Wait and see," my husband said cynically. "When you've got a 48 Charles to deal with, this may mean he's only plotting."

He seemed to be wrong. For over a week Charles was the 49 teacher's helper; each day he handed things out and he picked things up; no one had to stay after school.

"The P.T.A. meeting's next week again," I told my husband one 50 evening. "I'm going to find Charles's mother there."

"Ask her what happened to Charles," my husband said. "I'd like 51 to know."

"I'd like to know myself," I said. 52

On Friday of that week things were back to normal. "You know 53 what Charles did today?" Laurie demanded at the lunch table, in a voice slightly awed. "He told a little girl to say a word and she said it and the teacher washed her mouth out with soap and Charles laughed."

"What word?" his father asked unwisely, and Laurie said, "I'll 54 have to whisper it to you, it's so bad." He got down off his chair and went around to his father. His father bent his head down and Laurie whispered joyfully. His father's eyes widened.

"Did Charles tell the little girl to say *that*?" he asked respectfully. 55

"She said it *twice*," Laurie said. "Charles told her to say it *twice*." 56

"What happened to Charles?" my husband asked. 57

"Nothing," Laurie said. "He was passing out the crayons." 58

Monday morning Charles abandoned the little girl and said the   59
evil word himself three or four times, getting his mouth washed out
with soap each time. He also threw chalk.

My husband came to the door with me that evening as I set out for   60
the P.T.A. meeting. "Invite her over for a cup of tea after the meeting," he said. "I want to get a look at her."

"If only she's there," I said prayerfully.   61

"She'll be there," my husband said. "I don't see how they could   62
hold a P.T.A. meeting without Charles's mother."

At the meeting I sat restlessly, scanning each comfortable   63
matronly face, trying to determine which one hid the secret of
Charles. None of them looked to me haggard enough. No one stood
up in the meeting and apologized for the way her son had been acting.
No one mentioned Charles.

After the meeting I identified and sought out Laurie's kinder-   64
garten teacher. She had a plate with a cup of tea and a piece of chocolate cake; I had a plate with a cup of tea and a piece of marshmallow
cake. We maneuvered up to one another cautiously, and smiled.

"I've been so anxious to meet you," I said. "I'm Laurie's mother."   65

"We're all so interested in Laurie," she said.   66

"Well, he certainly likes kindergarten," I said. "He talks about it   67
all the time."

"We had a little trouble adjusting, the first week or so," she said   68
primly, "but now he's a fine little helper. With occasional lapses, of
course."

"Laurie usually adjusts very quickly," I said. "I suppose this time   69
it's Charles's influence."

"Charles?"   70

"Yes," I said laughing, "you must have your hands full in that   71
kindergarten, with Charles."

"Charles?" she said. "We don't have any Charles in the kinder-   72
garten."

Focusing on the Story

1. What is Laurie's attitude toward Charles and Charles's behavior? Support your answer with evidence from the story.
2. What does Laurie think will happen to Charles?
3. Describe Laurie's behavior at home. How is it similar to Charles's behavior at school?
4. How does Laurie explain why he is late on Monday? Why is he really late?
5. Laurie's mother worries that "kindergarten is unsettling for Laurie." Why does she worry about Charles's behavior?
6. Who is Laurie's mother looking for at the P.T.A. meeting? Does she find her? Who is Charles?

Interpreting and Evaluating

1. Why does Laurie make up stories about Charles? Is he a disturbed child who needs psychiatric treatment?
2. How should the parents handle Laurie's behavior? Should he be punished for lying?
3. What would you have done if Laurie had been your child?
4. Why is the title of the story "Charles" when the story is really about Laurie? Would another title such as "Laurie" be better? Why or why not?
5. Author Shirley Jackson has sprinkled many clues throughout the story as to who Charles really is. At what point in the story did you suspect Charles's identity?
6. Although author Shirley Jackson doesn't describe Laurie's personality directly, she shows it through Laurie's words and actions. What can you infer about the kind of child Laurie is?
7. Why is Laurie's mother so anxious to meet Charles's mother?
8. How do you think Laurie's mother feels when the teacher tells her that there is no Charles in kindergarten? How would you have felt if you had been Laurie's mother?
9. What advice do you think the teacher will give to Laurie's mother? What advice would you give the mother?

10. Do you think Laurie will eventually become a successful student? Is he smart? What career fields might be especially suited for him?
11. "A Mother in Mannville" by Marjorie Rawlings and "Charles" by Shirley Jackson both have surprise endings. Why do stories with surprise endings appeal to us?

Ideas for Writing and Further Discussion

1. Write a few paragraphs about a person you know well, such as a relative or a friend. Start with an overall impression of the person, and then instead of telling the reader what the person is like, show his or her personality through dialogue and action.
2. Write a narrative essay about a time when you blamed someone else for something you did. What did you do? Who did you blame, and what was the result?

   It's not necessary to write a formal thesis statement in a narrative essay, but you may wish to start with a general statement that introduces the event and expresses an attitude toward the experience.
3. Write a narrative essay about an amusing childhood experience. Describe what happened. Did it end well or in disaster?
4. Write a narrative essay about an amusing experience you as an adult had with a child. The child may have been your own child, a younger sibling or someone else's child. Describe what happened. How did it end?
5. Write a story of your own with a surprise ending. Start by establishing when and where the action takes place. Who are the characters or people involved in the story? What is the main problem and how is it resolved? What is the surprise? The story can be true or made up. It is not necessary to write a formal thesis statement in a narrative story of this kind, but you may wish to start with a general statement that introduces the event and expresses an attitude toward the experience.

An Additional Idea for Discussion and Writing

Discuss or write an essay in which you compare and/or contrast the writer in "A Mother in Mannville" by Marjorie Rawlings, Señora Ines in "The Stolen Party" by Liliana Heker, and the mother in "Charles" by Shirley Jackson. The end result will probably be a profile or a broad character sketch of three women who are far less perceptive than they think they are.

Suggested *thesis*: several ways in which they are similar or different.

Each *body paragraph* should explore one difference or similarity supported by examples from the stories.

Men
and
Women

❖

Love
and
Relationships

The Answer Is No

❖ •

Naguib Mahfouz

About the Author

Naguib Mahfouz is a well-known Egyptian author whose portrayal of life in present-day Egypt won him the Nobel Prize for Literature in 1988. His latest novel, *The Beginning and the End,* looks at the harsh life of ordinary Egyptians and in particular the plight of women. In addition to writing fiction, Naguib Mahfouz works as a journalist for the Egyptian newspaper *Al Ahram.*

Something to Think About

In some Third-World countries such as Egypt, the setting of the following story, a woman loses her prospects for marriage if she loses her virginity, even if she is raped. What do you think might be a woman's options if she finds herself in such a situation?

Words to Keep in Mind

headmaster *(1)* principal

decorously *(4)* politely; showing good taste in behavior, speech, and dress

attired *(4)* dressed

spherical *(4)* round

attained *(11)* achieved, gained

byword *(12)* one that is proverbial as a type of specified characteristics

rapacious *(12)* greedy

coercion *(13)* force

solitude *(13)* being alone

asperity *(14)* harshness or sharpness of temper

T he important piece of news that the new headmaster had arrived   1
spread through the school. She heard of it in the women teachers'
common room as she was casting a final glance at the day's lessons.
There was no getting away from joining the other teachers in congrat-
ulating him, and from shaking him by the hand too. A shudder passed
through her body, but it was unavoidable.

"They speak highly of his ability," said a colleague of hers. "And   2
they talk too of his strictness."

It had always been a possibility that might occur, and now it had.   3
Her pretty face paled, and a staring look came to her wide black eyes.

When the time came, the teachers went in single file, decorously   4
attired, to his open room. He stood behind his desk as he received the
men and women. He was of medium height, with a tendency to portli-
ness, and had a spherical face, hooked nose, and bulging eyes; the
first thing that could be seen of him was a thick, puffed-up mustache,
arched like a foam-laden wave. She advanced with her eyes fixed on
his chest. Avoiding his gaze, she stretched out her hand. What was she
to say? Just what the others had said? However, she kept silent,
uttered not a word. What, she wondered, did his eyes express? His
rough hand shook hers, and he said in a gruff voice, "Thanks." She
turned elegantly and moved off.

She forgot her worries through her daily tasks, though she did not   5
look in good shape. Several of the girls remarked, "Miss is in a bad
mood." When she returned to her home at the beginning of the

From *The Time and the Place and Other Stories* by Naguib Mahfouz. Translated by
Denys Johnson-Davies. © 1991 by the American University in Cairo Press. Used by
permission of Doubleday, a division of Random House, Inc.

Pyramids Road, she changed her clothes and sat down to eat with her mother. "Everything all right?" inquired her mother, looking her in the face.

"Badran, Badran Badawi," she said briefly. "Do you remember 6 him? He's been appointed our headmaster."

"Really!"   7

Then, after a moment of silence, she said, "It's of no importance 8 at all—it's an old and long-forgotten story."

After eating, she took herself off to her study to rest for a while 9 before correcting some exercise books. She had forgotten him completely. No, not completely. How could he be forgotten completely? When he had first come to give her a private lesson in mathematics, she was fourteen years of age. In fact not quite fourteen. He had been twenty-five years older, the same age as her father. She had said to her mother, "His appearance is a mess, but he explains things well." And her mother had said, "We're not concerned with what he looks like; what's important is how he explains things."

He was an amusing person, and she got on well with him and ben- 10 efited from his knowledge. How, then, had it happened? In her innocence she had not noticed any change in his behavior to put her on her guard. Then one day he had been left on his own with her, her father having gone to her aunt's clinic. She had not the slightest doubts about a man she regarded as a second father. How, then, had it happened? Without love or desire on her part the thing had happened. She had asked in terror about what had occurred, and he had told her, "Don't be frightened or sad. Keep it to yourself and I'll come and propose to you the day you come of age."

And he had kept his promise and had come to ask for her hand. 11 By then she had attained a degree of maturity that gave her an understanding of the dimensions of her tragic position. She had found that she had no love or respect for him and that he was as far as he could be from her dreams and from the ideas she had formed of what constituted an ideal and moral person. But what was to be done? Her father had passed away two years ago, and her mother had been taken aback by the forwardness of the man. However, she had said to her, "I know your attachment to your personal independence, so I leave the decision to you."

She had been conscious of the critical position she was in. She   12
had either to accept or to close the door forever. It was the sort of situation that could force her into something she detested. She was the
rich, beautiful girl, a byword in Abbasiyya for her nobility of character, and now here she was struggling helplessly in a well-sprung trap,
while he looked down at her with rapacious eyes. Just as she had
hated his strength, so too did she hate her own weakness. To have
abused her innocence was one thing, but for him to have the upper
hand now that she was fully in possession of her faculties was something else. He had said, "So here I am, making good my promise
because I love you." He had also said, "I know of your love of teaching, and you will complete your studies at the College of Science."

She had felt such anger as she had never felt before. She had   13
rejected coercion in the same way as she rejected ugliness. It had
meant little to her to sacrifice marriage. She had welcomed being on
her own, for solitude accompanied by self-respect was not loneliness.
She had also guessed he was after her money. She had told her mother
quite straightforwardly, "No," to which her mother had replied, "I am
astonished you did not make this decision from the first moment."

The man had blocked her way outside and said, "How can you   14
refuse? Don't you realize the outcome?" And she had replied with an
asperity he had not expected, "For me any outcome is preferable to
being married to you."

After finishing her studies, she had wanted something to do to fill   15
her spare time, so she had worked as a teacher. Chances to marry had
come time after time, but she had turned her back on them all.

"Does no one please you?" her mother asked her.   16

"I know what I'm doing," she had said gently.   17

"But time is going by."   18

"Let it go as it pleases, I am content."   19

Day by day she becomes older. She avoids love, fears it. With all   20
her strength she hopes that life will pass calmly, peacefully, rather
than happily. She goes on persuading herself that happiness is not
confined to love and motherhood. Never has she regretted her firm
decision. Who knows what the morrow holds? But she was certainly
unhappy that he should again make his appearance in her life, that she

would be dealing with him day after day, and that he would be making of the past a living and painful present.

Then, the first time he was alone with her in his room, he asked 21 her, "How are you?"

She answered coldly, "I'm fine." 22

He hesitated slightly before inquiring, "Have you not . . . I mean, 23 did you get married?"

In the tone of someone intent on cutting short a conversation, she 24 said, "I told you, I'm fine."

Focusing on the Story

1. Describe the main character. Is she attractive and educated? What is her economic status?
2. From where does the main character know the new headmaster, Badran Badawi? What had their relationship been?
3. What crime had been committed against the main character when she was about fourteen? Why didn't she tell her parents about the incident? Did she report it to the police?
4. Why is the main character's mother astonished that the daughter takes so long to refuse the old tutor's marriage proposal? Similarly, why is she at a loss when her daughter refuses other marriage proposals?

Interpreting and Evaluating

1. The author, Naguib Mahfouz, has not given the main character a name. What may be some reasons for this omission?
2. After the main character has made her decision not to marry her old tutor, the tutor asks incredulously, "How can you refuse? Don't you realize the outcome?" What does the old tutor mean? Considering that in the Moslem culture a woman loses her opportunity for marriage when she loses her virginity, do you think it is a difficult decision for the main character? Explain.
3. Why does the main character avoid and fear love? Is her fear necessarily based on cultural restrictions alone?

4. Why is rape a particularly heinous crime? What are some emotional scars that rape may leave?
5. To what does the title "The Answer Is No" refer? Give examples of several "no's" in the answer.
6. The main character tries to persuade herself that "happiness is not confined to love and motherhood." Is a woman's happiness confined to love and motherhood, in your opinion? Explain.

Ideas for Writing and Further Discussion

1. Why do some men commit crimes specifically against women? What, if anything, in their background and personality could account for such acts? Write an essay in which you explore reasons why men commit such crimes.
   Suggested *thesis*: two or three such reasons.
   Each *body paragraph* should discuss one reason.
2. What are some career options women have today that were not available to our mothers and grandmothers? Write an essay in which you compare and contrast the choices available to our mothers and grandmothers with the choices women have today.
   Suggested *thesis*: several areas that are open to women today that were not open to our mothers and grandmothers.
   Each *body paragraph* might compare and contrast one area. Or, one body paragraph might deal with the few areas open to our mothers and grandmothers. Two other body paragraphs might then deal with two different areas open to women today.

Butterfly Man

❖

The Maidu Indians
(recorded by Dr. Roland Dixon)

About the Authors

The Maidu Indians made their home in northeastern California between the Sacramento River and the Sierras. Dr. Roland Dixon made several trips to study the Maidu and recorded many of their stories. "Butterfly Man" was recorded sometime around 1900.

Something to Think About

What will happen to a woman who leaves her baby to run after butterflies that turn out to be beautiful men in disguise?

Words to Keep in Mind

tabu *(1)* something forbidden by tradition (taboo)

cradleboard *(2)* used by Native American women to transport babies

manzanita *(4)* evergreen shrub common in northeastern California

dentalium shell *(10)* tooth shell

abalone shell *(10)* pretty shell, slightly spiral in form and lined with mother-of-pearl

I t was springtime along the river and Tolowim-Woman was restless   1
and lonely. Tolowim-Man was downriver spearing salmon. She knew

that when he came home, he would join the other men in the sweat house. This was the time of the spring deer drive, the time when a woman is unclean and is avoided by her husband if he is taking part in the drive. Tolowim-Man must keep himself absolutely pure now for he was one of those who would impersonate the deer, and this is a dangerous thing to do at best. This was the time for a good wife to stay indoors and to help to see that no tabu was broken.

Tolowim-Woman was a good wife, but she remembered that 2 spring is also the time when wild iris blooms in the hills. And Tolowim-Woman was weary of women's gossip and women's voices. So, she settled her basket hat straight on her head and let herself quietly out of her house by way of the low front passage. She took care not to jiggle or disturb the baby on his cradleboard at her back.

Once outside she stood erect, gazed briefly up and down the river, 3 then turned away from it and walked up into the hills.

The sun was bright and hot. After walking for some time 4 Tolowim-Woman, out of breath, slipped the carrying strap from her forehead and put the cradleboard in the shade of a manzanita bush and sat down to rest.

As she sat, a butterfly fluttered softly by. It brushed the baby's 5 arm, causing him to laugh and try to touch it.

It brushed Tolowim-Woman's cheek and she too laughed and 6 tried to touch it. It settled for a moment on a branch of the manzanita bush, and Tolowim-Woman, laughing again, stretched quickly forward to cover it with her seed basket. But it fluttered on to the next bush, just out of her reach. She got up from the ground, following and trying to capture it.

She wanted this butterfly as she had not wanted anything for a 7 long, long time. It was large and strong-flying as butterflies rarely are, and it was very beautiful, with wing bands black as the mussel's shell and stripes scarlet as the woodpecker's crest.

The butterfly was so little ahead of her that each new step or 8 reach seemed to be the one that would capture it. But always it kept its free fluttering way, just ahead, just out of reach. Nor was it flying

From *The Inland Whale* by Theodora Kroeber. © 1959, reprinted by permission of Indiana University Press, Bloomington.

at random, for its start-and-stop course was leading her ever up and back, farther into the hills, farther from the river.

Tolowim-Woman looked back at the baby, sleepy and comfort- 9 able in the shade of the manzanita bush. She had come a long way from him. The butterfly would tire soon now. She would make a last try for it over this next hill and take it back to the baby.

But the butterfly did not tire nor did it allow itself to be captured. 10 Tolowim-Woman became so intent on possessing it that through the long afternoon it led her on and on. Her buckskin skirt was dirty and torn from the thorny bushes. Her cap was brushed from her head, and she did not stop to pick it up. And the heavy strings of polished dentalium and abalone shell about her neck were broken, scattered and lost.

At last as the sun was setting, and far inland, among hills she did 11 not know, Tolowim-Woman sank exhausted to the ground. The butterfly turned at once, and fluttered back to her. It came and settled down beside her. In the dusk she saw that it had become a swift and graceful man, naked save for the butterfly girdle encircling his waist, his long hair held in a black and red headband.

Together they passed the night, Tolowim-Woman and Butterfly 12 Man. In the morning, Butterfly Man asked her, "You wish to go with me?"

She answered, "Yes! I do." 13

Then he said to her, "That is good. One more day's travelling will 14 bring us to my land, and there we shall live. But it is a long and dangerous way, O my Wife. We must cross the Valley of Butterflies and they will try to take you from me. Will you do as I say that I may lead you safely through?"

She promised to do as he told her. He said, "Follow close behind 15 me. Step where I step. Hold tight with both your hands to my girdle. Do not let go even for a moment. And do not look at any butterfly until we are out of the valley. Obey me for this time and you shall be forever safe. Remember, I lose my power to protect you if you haven't your hands on my girdle."

They started off, Butterfly Man in the lead, Tolowim-Woman fol- 16 lowing. She grasped the girdle firmly in both her hands and she looked only at the ground. In this manner they came to the Valley of Butterflies and travelled some distance into it.

It was rough underfoot and Butterfly Man set a straight, fast   17
course—down, across, up.

Butterflies hovered on the rocks over which they had to step.   18
Butterflies caught against their legs and in their hair and fluttered
before their faces. The air of the valley seemed to be entirely filled
with butterflies.

For a long time Tolowim-Woman remembered to keep her hands   19
on the girdle and her eyes on the pathless way underfoot. But then a
butterfly, all black, larger even than Butterfly Man had been, and
shining as the crow, hovered before her. He hovered just above her
breasts in the line of her downcast eyes and settled for a long moment
on her lips. Then he flew slowly away. She gasped with the excitement of his beauty. Her eyes followed his flight and she took one
hand off the girdle and reached greedily for him.

He was gone.   20

But at once a hundred, a thousand others danced before her,   21
against her eyes and cheeks and mouth. They were black and pure
white and pale gold and swamp green and iris purple.

She wanted them all, and she let go her hold on Butterfly Man's   22
girdle and reached for them with both her hands.

Not one could she catch.   23

Butterfly Man did not stop or look back. She kept him in sight for   24
a time, but as she clutched ever more wildly at one and then another,
she fell far, far behind him.

She ran after this butterfly and that one, here and there, up and   25
down, stumbling, desperate, at random, always reaching for another
one and always missing it.

Her hair was unbraided and tangled, her skirt kept catching in the   26
bushes and holding her back. She untied it and threw it away. Her
moccasins were in shreds. Naked except for her bark apron, dishev-
elled, obsessed, she continued her hopeless chase.

Butterfly Man was gone now. He was across the valley and in his   27
own land.

Tolowim-Woman followed one butterfly and then another, on and   28
on and on. And then her heart went away, and this was the end of
Tolowim-Woman.

Focusing on the Story

1. When must Tolowim-Man stay away from his wife according to this story?
2. What are some important sources of food for the Tolowim Indian tribe, an imaginary tribe made up by the Maidu Indians?
3. Describe Tolowim-Woman as she is leaving her house and walking into the hills. What is she wearing? What does she take with her?
4. With whom does Tolowim-Woman spend the night in the hills? What does her companion tell her to do so that he "may lead [her] safely through" the Valley of Butterflies?
5. What happens when a shiny black butterfly hovers "just above her breasts in the line of her downcast eyes"? Does Tolowim-Woman catch him? Does she catch any of the other butterflies?
6. What happens to Tolowim-Woman in the end?

Interpreting and Evaluating

1. Why does Tolowim-Woman decide to leave her house and go into the hills? Why does she become so obsessed with the butterflies?
2. What might the butterflies represent? Give evidence from the story to support your opinion. How is the ending inevitable?
3. Tolowim-Woman leaves her baby under a bush to chase the butterflies. What does this action say about her sense of responsibility? What other inferences can you make about her character from the story?
4. If this is a morality tale, a cautionary tale, or a fable, what is the moral of the story?
5. The story was told by the Maidu Indians, but the events in the story occur among the imaginary Tolowim tribe outside the Maidu world. What may be the reason for having the characters be outsiders?

Ideas for Writing and Further Discussion

1. The Butterfly Man may have been the product of a woman's daydreaming. What evidence can you find in the story for such an

interpretation? What in Indian lore may lend support to the fact that this story is a woman's fantasy? For example, the Indian women had to spend much time alone. Furthermore, it was the women who gathered berries, fruit, and nuts in the California hills, which are often alive with colorful butterflies. Finally, what traits does a butterfly possess that may fuel a woman's fantasy of a beautiful man in disguise?

Write an essay in which you discuss several reasons why the story "Butterfly Man" may be bedded in a woman's imagination. Use the above suggestions as well as others of your own to develop your essay.

Suggested *thesis*: two or three reasons why "Butterfly Man" may be a product of a woman's fantasy.

Each *body paragraph* should provide supporting details for one such reason.

2. The grass is always greener on the other side of the fence, according to an old saying. Have you ever tried to go after something that you didn't have at the expense of something that you already had?

   Write a paragraph or two about a time when you sacrificed something you had for something you desired. Describe what happened. What was the outcome? Did you learn anything from the experience?

The Cock

❖

Tao Kim Hai

About the Author

Tao Kim Hai, a Vietnamese journalist and short story writer, is known in French literary circles. Tao Kim Hai has written several books on former French Indo-China.

Something to Think About

Do you have a favorite possession that has a special meaning just to you? Why is it special?

Words to Keep in Mind

betel *(1)* a pepper tree whose leaves are chewed with lime and betel nut as a stimulant in Southeast Asia

conjugal *(2)* related to the sexual aspect of marriage

crop *(2)* wide part of the throat or neck of a bird

deposed *(2)* removed from a throne or other high position

spurs *(2)* sharp spines on the foot of a game cock used for slashing his opponent

monochord *(4)* instrument with one string

paddy *(6)* rice in the husk

trysting-place *(8)* lovers' secret meeting place

lethal *(12)* deadly

saber *(12)* sword

palaver *(14)* long discussion

tête-a-tête *(14)* intimate meeting

prostrate *(14)* to lie face down in submission or adoration

barge *(16)* flat-bottomed boat usually towed

piastres (16) unit of currency in former South Vietnam

Y ou're quite right; he has certainly outlived his usefulness, and we   1
should kill him. But my husband would never agree to it, and neither
would I. Help yourself to betel again, honored sister, and I will tell
you why.

Yes, he's getting quite old for a rooster, and he doesn't perform   2
his conjugal duties as he should. But there's no question of killing
him, nor even of giving his harem to a younger cock. In the first
place, he'd fight until his crop was torn open rather than be deposed.
He comes of fighting stock—see how long and sharp his spurs are,
and how they curve. And in spite of his age, he's still fast enough on
his feet to defend his rights. His feet are his most aristocratic feature;
notice how the scales grow in two straight lines like the Chinese mot-
toes on either side of a door, with not a sign of a feather between
them. His mother was only an ordinary Cochin-China hen, but his sire
was a real Cambodian fighting cock with I've no idea how many
fights to his credit. But that's neither here nor there; it's not for his
fighting blood that I value him. The truth is that he did me a great service five years ago. It's thanks to my poor old rooster that I married
the man I love.

Five years ago, my husband lived next door to my parents. We   3
were neighbors, but the distance between us was immeasurable,
unbridgeable. He had neither father nor mother; my father was the *ly-
truong* (mayor) of the community. His house was a little hut built on
date-palm posts, walled with bamboo and thatched with water-palm
leaves; my house had four rows of carved teakwood columns, walls

From *Asia Magazine,* March 1946. United Nations World. Translated by Ruth Barber.

of whitewashed brick and a red-tiled roof. My father had twenty oxen and ten buffaloes, and a thousand acres of rice fields; *he* hadn't even a patch of ground, and raised only a few chickens. To tell the truth, he was our *ta-diên* (tenant farmer).

Tenant or no, he was the handsomest young man, the best mono- 4 chord player and the fastest rice planter of the whole district. You should have heard him play the monochord in those days; it was enough to bring a goddess down from heaven. I've made him give up playing since we've been married, although I love music myself. It wasn't all because I was jealous of his monochord; I was afraid for his eyesight, too. Everybody says the monochord causes blindness, and the better the musician, the greater the danger.

He was eighteen, and I was two years younger. We were in love, 5 and our love was all the stronger because it was hopeless. An irresistible attraction drew me to him, in spite of his rough farm clothes and his unkempt hair.

In his poultry yard a young cock with green and gold plumage 6 and a blood-red comb lorded it over the admiring hens. He fought all the other cocks in the village, and gallantly refused the paddy and broken rice thrown to his little flock until his wives had eaten their fill. He was brave, and he was not at all bashful, either with the hens or before me. You would have said he took a wicked delight in making love to them in my presence. Then he would cock a glittering eye at me, and crow.

One day his master and I were talking behind the bamboo hut, 7 where we were safe from all indiscreet eyes. Suddenly we heard a loud "Ha, ha, ha!" We turned around in alarm; it was only the cock. My suitor threw a stick at him. He saw it coming and made a magnificent leap to one side, so that the stick only grazed his tail. Then with an indignant "Kut-kut-kut" he stalked off to rejoin his hens, looking for all the world like an insulted sovereign. From the safety of the poultry yard he looked back at us, and, like a practical joker who has just pulled off a good one, he crowed, "Ha, ha, ha, ha-a-a-!"

Another day we had found a trysting-place at the foot of a big 8 straw-stack, from which we could look out over the endless reaches of my father's rice fields, the obstacle to our marriage. That accursed cock came and perched on top of the straw-stack, discovered us and, beating his wings in the air as if to call the whole world to witness, he let out a scandalized "Oh-oh-oh-rooo!"

In trying to chase the old tattle-tale away, we lost all sense of cau-   9 tion, and he was not the only one to see us together that time. Soon the village was buzzing with gossip about us; the cock had set tongues wagging. Jealous girls, and young men too, whispered that I had lost my virtue, and the old *bagia* shook their heads and began to speculate on the date when my figure would show the results of my fall. And of course the rumors did not fail to reach my parents' ears.

The cock joined the other gossips. No longer satisfied to crow all   10 day, he started to crow in the evening, too, after the lamps were lit. His competitors, a thousand times outcrowed but still ambitious, replied from all the henhouses of the village. You never heard such a racket.

Do you believe here in your province, honorable elder sister, that   11 the crowing of a cock in the evening is the sign of an extramarital pregnancy? In our district everybody believed it, even my mother. My poor mother is superstitious. In spite of my tears and my denials, she took me for a lost virgin who dared not acknowledge her fall. No need for *me* to admit it; the cocks were there to proclaim it far and wide.

My grandparents were summoned, and my aunts and uncles on   12 my mother's side and on my father's. They shut me up in my little room and held a family caucus in the living room before the altar of our ancestors. I thought my last hour was come, and I waited for them to bring me the lethal cup, the saber and the red silk cord. Which death should I choose—poisoning, bleeding or hanging? Would they shave my head like a nun's before they forced me to commit suicide? Suicide it certainly must be, for the family of a mayor must never lose face.

But I was an only child, and my mother was already old. No mat-   13 ter what the sacrifice, the family must have another generation to carry on the cult of the ancestors. If I were to die without issue, my mother would be forced to choose a concubine for my father and to admit her to the marriage bed, to cherish the concubine's children as her own. Then, too, I suspect that my father was beginning to be influenced by European ideas. Above all, he loved me a great deal, although the traditional reserve that a father must observe toward his daughter kept him from showing it. Whatever the reason, the family council decided to do nothing worse than to marry me off in all haste. And to whom, God in Heaven? To my seducer, no less. I agreed without a murmur.

The six preliminary marriage ceremonies were gotten through 14 with before two weeks had passed, and we were married in the strictest privacy. The formal proposal was without pomp and palaver; the betel ceremony was reduced to little more than a tête-a-tête in everyday clothes. As for the suitor's period of probation in the house of his future wife, which usually lasts from six months to two years, we simply omitted it. No invitations on scarlet paper with gold script, no official delegation from the town council, no gift of ring-necked ducks on a brass platter, no open-air banquet lasting far into the night. But there were also none of those more or less annoying jokes which most young couples have to resign themselves to—the drinking party in the bridal chamber, the bed that rocks, the bridegroom who is kidnapped. We had only to prostrate ourselves, I in a wide-sleeved red dress and he in a black tunic and turban, before the altars of our ancestors and before my parents, less to ask their benediction than to make honorable amends.

It was a bad match, and a scandalous one; the less said the better.   15

It had been agreed that we should leave our native village imme- 16 diately and make our home in some distant province where we were not known. On our wedding night we set out on the long journey, in a big barge that my parents had loaded with rice, salt fish, and *piastres*. We were accompanied by two faithful servants and the cock, who followed us into exile with all his little harem.

We've been here for five years now, honorable sister, in your rich 17 and peaceful province, and as you know, we haven't yet had a child. My poor mother writes me that she spends her days running to the pagodas having prayers said and sacrifices made, in the hope of becoming a grandmother before she goes to join her ancestors at the Golden Spring. The poor old cock has been proved a liar. But thanks to his lies I'm a happy woman, and he shall have all the white rice he can eat to the end of his days.

Focusing on the Story

1. Where is the narrator (the character who tells the story), and to whom is she talking?
2. Why is the rooster so special to the narrator? What does it symbolize?
3. Why was the narrator attracted to the young man? What were the basic obstacles to their marriage?
4. When the family discovered the secret relationship between the narrator and her boyfriend, the relatives were summoned, and they "held a family caucus in the living room before the altar of [the] ancestors." What was often expected of a daughter who disgraced the family in this or any other way? What awful choices would the narrator have had if her family had brought her "the lethal cup, the saber, and the red silk cord"?
5. There are hints of several superstitious beliefs in the story. Name at least two.

Interpreting and Evaluating

1. Why was the narrator allowed to marry her suitor after all? Why did the newlyweds have to leave the village? Is the narrator happy? Are the parents happy? Give evidence from the story to support your opinion.
2. Did the narrator's parents do the right thing by sending their daughter and son-in-law away? Should they have been less influenced by the social pressure of the town in which they lived? How can tradition and social pressure be both good and bad?
3. If the narrator had married someone of her own status, elaborate ceremonies would have been planned. Did the narrator miss out on a great party, or did she escape a dreadful ordeal?
4. Although the setting is Vietnam, the basic story plot (what's happening in the story) is similar to many Western stories. What other stories have you read or seen on television or in the movies that have similar story lines or plots?
5. Even under the most ideal circumstances, marriage can be a difficult undertaking. How can marriage become even more difficult if the

partners are from different backgrounds? How can these difficulties be overcome?

Ideas for Writing and Further Discussion

1. Do you have a favorite possession with a special symbolic significance? Write a paragraph describing such a possession, and explain why it is special. Begin with a general sentence that expresses your attitude toward the object.

2. As the saying goes, forbidden fruit tastes sweetest. If you agree, take a stand and write an essay in which you give examples from your own experience that prove this saying to be true.
   Suggested *thesis*: two or three examples that support your stand.
   Each *body paragraph* should look at one example and show how it proves the above saying to be true.

3. Are you superstitious? Do you knock on wood? Do you avoid walking under a ladder? Why do you think people are superstitious? Write an essay in which you describe some common superstitions that people you know believe in.
   Suggested *thesis*: two or three such superstitions.
   Each *body paragraph* should describe one superstition and explain why people believe in it and how it affects them.

Difficulty
with a Bouquet

❖

William Sansom

About the Author

William Sansom was a British writer who wrote about life in his native London. He died in 1976.

Something to Think About

When was the last time you did something nice for a fellow human without expecting anything in return? Why are we suspicious of people who want to give us gifts for no apparent reason? What has happened to simple brotherhood (or sisterhood) in our fast-paced society?

Words to Keep in Mind

chestnuts *(2)* trees with large leaves

hollyhocks *(2)* tall plants with large flowers of various colors

ulterior *(6)* hidden

affectation *(6)* artificial behavior intended to impress others

aggrandizement *(7)* increase in power or wealth

seduction *(7)* tempting someone to do something wrong, especially sexually

motive *(7)* an inner drive or impulse that causes a person to act in a certain way

flinched *(8)* drew back as a show of weakness; winced

bravados *(8)* pretended couragous acts

maudlin *(11)* sentimental

Seal, walking through his garden, said suddenly to himself: "I would like to pick some flowers and take them to Miss D." 1

The afternoon was light and warm. Tall chestnuts fanned themselves in a pleasant breeze. Among the hollyhocks there was a good humming as the bees tumbled from flower to flower. Seal wore an open shirt. He felt fresh and fine, with the air swimming coolly under his shirt and around his ribs. The summer's afternoon was free. Nothing pressed him. It was a time when some simple, disinterested impulse might well be hoped to flourish. 2

Seal felt a great joy in the flowers around him and from this a brilliant longing to give. He wished to give quite inside himself, uncritically, without thinking for a moment: "Here am I, Seal, wishing something." Seal merely wanted to give some of his flowers to a fellow being. It had happened that Miss D was the first person to come to mind. He was in no way attached to Miss D. He knew her slightly, as a plain, elderly girl of about twenty who had come to live in the flats opposite his garden. If Seal had ever thought about Miss D at all, it was because he disliked the way she walked. She walked stiffly, sailing with her long body while her little legs raced to catch up with it. But he was not thinking of this now. Just by chance he had glimpsed the block of flats as he had stooped to pick a flower. The flats had presented the image of Miss D to his mind. 3

Seal chose common, ordinary flowers. As the stems broke he whistled between his teeth. He had chosen these ordinary flowers because they were the nearest to hand: in the second place, because 4 they were fresh and full of life. They were neither rare nor costly. They were pleasant, fresh, unassuming flowers.

With the flowers in his hand, Seal walked contentedly from his ⁵ garden and set foot on the asphalt pavement that led to the block of flats across the way. But as his foot touched the asphalt, as the sly glare of an old man fixed his eye for the moment of its passing, as the traffic asserted itself, certain misgivings began to freeze his impromptu joy. "Good heavens," he suddenly thought, "what am I doing?" He stepped outside himself and saw Seal carrying a bunch of cheap flowers to Miss D in the flats across the way.

"These are cheap flowers," he thought. "This is a sudden gift; I ⁶ shall smile as I hand them to her. We shall both know that there is no ulterior reason for the gift and thus the whole action will smack of goodness—of goodness and simple brotherhood. And somehow . . . for that reason this gesture of mine will appear to be the most calculated pose of all. Such a simple gesture is improbable. The improbable is to be suspected. My gift will certainly be regarded as an affectation.

"Oh, if only I had some reason—aggrandizement, financial gain, ⁷ seduction—any of the accepted motives that would return my flowers to social favor. But no—I have none of these in me. I only wish to give and to receive nothing in return."

As he walked on, Seal could see himself bowing and smiling. He ⁸ saw himself smile too broadly as he apologized by exaggeration for his good action. His neck flinched with disgust as he saw himself assume the old bravados. He could see the mocking smile of recognition on the face of Miss D.

Seal dropped the flowers into the gutter and walked slowly back ⁹ to his garden.

From her window high up in the concrete flats, Miss D watched ¹⁰ Seal drop the flowers. How fresh they looked! How they would have livened her barren room! "Wouldn't it have been nice," thought Miss D, "if that Mr. Seal had been bringing *me* that pretty bouquet of flowers! Wouldn't it have been nice if he had picked them in his own garden and—well, just brought them along, quite casually, and made me a present of the delightful afternoon." Miss D dreamed on for a few minutes.

Then she frowned, rose, straightened her suspender belt, hurried   11
into the kitchen. "Thank God he didn't," she sighed to herself. "I
should have been most embarrassed. It's not as if he wanted me. It
would have been just too maudlin for words."

Focusing on the Story

1. Describe Miss D. Is she attractive? Where does she live? How
   would you describe her lifestyle?
2. How would you describe Seal's relationship with Miss D? Is he in
   love with her?
3. What are some of Seal's thoughts as he steps "outside himself and
   [sees himself] carrying a bunch of cheap flowers to Miss D in the
   flats across the way"?
4. What are Miss D's first thoughts when she sees Seal drop the flowers in the gutter?

Interpreting and Evaluating

1. Why does Seal want to give flowers to Miss D? Why do "common,
   ordinary flowers" seem appropriate?
2. Why does Seal think his gift will be "regarded as an affectation,"
   and why will his friendly gesture seem calculated and suspicious?
3. After watching Seal drop the flowers, Miss D "frowned, rose,
   straightened her suspender belt, hurried into the kitchen. 'Thank
   God he didn't,' she sighed to herself. 'I should have been most
   embarrassed.'" Why would she have been embarrassed if Seal had
   given her the flowers?
4. Irony is the difference between what is expected and what actually
   happens. What is ironic in this story?
5. What are some common occasions for giving gifts? Would any of
   them apply to Seal?
6. Seal says that his gift of flowers will "smack of goodness . . . and
   simple brotherhood," so he tosses the flowers in the gutter. Why is a
   simple good deed to be suspected today? Have we as a society lost
   something valuable? Explain.

Idea for Writing or Further Discussion

What kinds of gifts do you like to give? When do you like to give gifts? Write about different occasions when you give presents in your family. Give examples of gifts that are appropriate for each occasion.

Suggested *thesis*: three or four of your favorite occasions for giving gifts.

Each *body paragraph* should discuss one such occasion and give examples of gifts appropriate for that occasion.

The Gift of the Magi

❖

O. Henry

About the Author

O. Henry, a pseudonym for William Sydney Porter, was an American short story writer whose stories depict life in New York during the first decade of the twentieth century. Many of O. Henry's stories have been translated into dozens of languages.

Something to Think About

It's been said that the best things in life are free. What does this mean?

Words to Keep in Mind

magi *(title)* three wise men of the East who brought gifts for baby Jesus

imputation of parsimony *(1)* feeling that people think you are stingy

beggar *(3)* to seem inadequate

mendicancy squad *(3)* police squad charged with chasing away beggars

vestibule *(4)* hallway

appertaining *(4)* belonging

pier-glass *(7)* tall mirror set in a wall between windows

Queen of Sheba *(9)* queen from South Arabia known for her beauty

King Solomon *(9)* king of Israel famous for his wealth and wisdom cascade *(10)* waterfall

hashed *(18)* spoiled by clumsy work

metaphor *(18)* figure of speech

fob *(19)* small chain attached to a pocket watch

chaste *(19)* pure, simple in design

meretricious *(19)* too showy or flashy

prudence *(20)* caution

quail *(26)* kind of game bird

enfolded *(34)* embraced, hugged

inconsequential *(34)* unimportant

assertion *(34)* statement

illuminated *(34)* explained

tresses *(38)* long locks of hair

coveted *(38)* longed for with envy

One dollar and eighty-seven cents. That was all. And 60 cents of it 1
was in pennies. Pennies saved one and two at a time by bulldozing the
grocer and the vegetable man and the butcher until one's cheeks
burned with the silent imputation of parsimony that such close dealing implied. Three times Della counted it. One dollar and eighty-
seven cents. And the next day would be Christmas.

There was clearly nothing to do but flop down on the shabby little 2
couch and howl. So Della did it. Which instigates the moral reflection
that life is made up of sobs, sniffles and smiles, with sniffles predom-
inating.

While the mistress of the home is gradually subsiding from the 3
first stage to the second, take a look at the home. A furnished flat at $8
per week. It did not exactly beggar description, but it certainly had
that word on the lookout for the mendicancy squad.

In the vestibule below belonged to this flat a letter-box into which 4
no letter would go, and an electric button from which no mortal finger

First published in *New York Sunday World Magazine,* December 10, 1905.

could coax a ring. Also appertaining thereunto was a card bearing the name "Mr. James Dillingham Young."

The "Dillingham" had been flung to the breeze during a former 5 period of prosperity when its possessor was being paid $30 per week. Now, when the income was shrunk to $20, the letters of "Dillingham" looked blurred, as though they were thinking seriously of contracting to a modest and unassuming D. But whenever Mr. James Dillingham Young came home and reached his flat above he was called "Jim" and greatly hugged by Mrs. James Dillingham Young, already introduced to you as Della. Which is all very good.

Della finished her cry and attended to her cheeks with the powder 6 rag. She stood by the window and looked out dully at a gray cat walking a gray fence in a gray backyard. Tomorrow would be Christmas Day, and she had only $1.87 with which to buy Jim a present. She had been saving every penny she could for months, with this result. Twenty dollars a week doesn't go far. Expenses had been greater than she had calculated. They always are. Only $1.87 to buy a present for Jim. Her Jim. Many a happy hour she had spent planning for something nice for him. Something fine and rare and sterling—something just a little bit near to being worthy of the honor of being owned by Jim.

There was a pier-glass between the windows of the room. Perhaps 7 you have seen a pier-glass in an $8 flat. A very thin and very agile person may, by observing his reflection in a rapid sequence of longitudinal strips, obtain a fairly accurate conception of his looks. Della, being slender, had mastered the art.

Suddenly she whirled from the window and stood before the 8 glass. Her eyes were shining brilliantly, but her face had lost its color within twenty seconds. Rapidly she pulled down her hair and let it fall to its full length.

Now, there were two possessions of the James Dillingham 9 Youngs in which they both took a mighty pride. One was Jim's gold watch that had been his father's and his grandfather's. The other was Della's hair. Had the Queen of Sheba lived in the flat across the airshaft Della would have let her hair hang out the window some day to dry and mocked at Her Majesty's jewels and gifts. Had King Solomon been the janitor, with all his treasures piled up in the basement, Jim would have pulled out his watch every time he passed, just to see him pluck at his beard from envy.

So now Della's beautiful hair fell about her, rippling and shining   10 like a cascade of brown waters. It reached below her knee and made itself almost a garment for her. And then she did it up again nervously and quickly. Once she faltered for a minute and stood still while a tear or two splashed on the worn red carpet.

On went her old brown jacket; on went her old brown hat. With a   11 whirl of skirts and with the brilliant sparkle still in her eyes, she fluttered out the door and down the stairs to the street.

Where she stopped the sign read: "Mme. Sofronie. Hair Goods of   12 All Kinds." One flight up Della ran, and collected herself, panting, before Madame, large, too white, chilly and hardly looking the "Sofronie."

"Will you buy my hair?" asked Della.   13

"I buy hair," said Madame. "Take yer hat off and let's have a sight   14 at the looks of it."

Down rippled the brown cascade.   15

"Twenty dollars," said Madame, lifting the mass with a practised   16 hand.

"Give it to me quick," said Della.   17

Oh, and the next two hours tripped by on rosy wings. Forget the   18 hashed metaphor. She was ransacking the stores for Jim's present.

She found it at last. It surely had been made for Jim and no one   19 else. There was none other like it in any of the stores, and she had turned all of them inside out. It was a platinum fob chain simple and chaste in design, properly proclaiming its value by substance alone and not by meretricious ornamentation—as all good things should do. It was even worthy of The Watch. As soon as she saw it she knew that it must be Jim's. It was like him. Quietness and value—the description applied to both. Twenty-one dollars they took from her for it, and she hurried home with the 87 cents. With that chain on his watch Jim might be properly anxious about the time in any company. Grand as the watch was, he sometimes looked at it on the sly on account of the old leather strap that he used in place of a chain.

When Della reached home her intoxication gave way a little to   20
prudence and reason. She got out her curling irons and lighted the gas
and went to work repairing the ravages made by generosity added to
love. Which is always a tremendous task, dear friends—a mammoth
task.

Within forty minutes her head was covered with tiny, close-lying   21
curls that made her look wonderfully like a truant schoolboy. She
looked at her reflection in the mirror long, carefully and critically.

"If Jim doesn't kill me," she said to herself, "before he takes a   22
second look at me, he'll say I look like a Coney Island chorus girl.
But what could I do—oh, what could I do with a dollar and eighty-
seven cents!"

At 7 o'clock the coffee was made and the frying pan was on the   23
back of the stove hot and ready to cook the chops.

Jim was never late. Della doubled the fob chain in her hand and   24
sat on the corner of the table near the door that he always entered.
Then she heard his step on the stair away down on the first flight, and
she turned white for just a moment. She had a habit of saying little
silent prayers about the simplest everyday things, and now she whispered: "Please, God, make him think I am still pretty."

The door opened and Jim stepped in and closed it. He looked thin   25
and very serious. Poor fellow, he was only twenty-two—and to be
burdened with a family! He needed a new overcoat and he was without gloves.

Jim stopped inside the door, as immovable as a setter at the scent   26
of quail. His eyes were fixed upon Della, and there was an expression
in them that she could not read, and it terrified her. It was not anger,
nor surprise, nor disapproval, nor horror, nor any of the sentiments
that she had been prepared for. He simply stared at her fixedly with
that peculiar expression on his face.

Della wriggled off the table and went for him.   27

"Jim, darling," she cried, "don't look at me that way. I had my   28
hair cut off and sold it because I couldn't have lived through
Christmas without giving you a present. It'll grow again—you won't
mind, will you? I just had to do it. My hair grows awfully fast. Say

'Merry Christmas!' Jim, and let's be happy. You don't know what a
nice—what a beautiful, nice gift I've got for you."

"You've cut off your hair?" asked Jim, laboriously, as if he had   29
not arrived at that patent fact yet even after the hardest mental labor.

"Cut it off and sold it," said Della. "Don't you like me just as   30
well, anyhow? I'm me without my hair, ain't I?"

Jim looked about the room curiously.   31

"You say your hair is gone?" he said, with an air almost of idiocy.   32

"You needn't look for it," said Della. "It's sold, I tell you—sold   33
and gone too. It's Christmas Eve, boy. Be good to me, for it went for
you. Maybe the hairs of my head were numbered," she went on with a
sudden serious sweetness, "but nobody could ever count my love for
you. Shall I put the chops on, Jim?"

Out of his trance Jim seemed to quickly wake. He enfolded his   34
Della. For ten seconds let us regard with discreet scrutiny some
inconsequential object in the other direction. Eight dollars a week or a
million a year—what is the difference? A mathematician or a wit
would give you the wrong answer. The magi brought valuable gifts,
but that was not among them. This dark assertion will be illuminated
later on.

Jim drew a package from his overcoat pocket and threw it upon   35
the table.

"Don't make any mistake, Dell," he said, "about me. I don't think   36
there's anything in the way of a haircut or a shave or a shampoo that
could make me like my girl any less. But if you'll unwrap that package you may see why you had me going awhile at first."

White fingers and nimble tore at the string and paper. And then an   37
ecstatic scream of joy; and then, alas! a quick feminine change to hys-
terical tears and wails, necessitating the immediate employment of all
the comforting powers of the lord of the flat.

For there lay The Combs—the set of combs, side and back, that   38
Della had worshipped for long in a Broadway window. Beautiful
combs, pure tortoise shell, with jewelled rims—just the shade to wear
in the beautiful vanished hair. They were expensive combs, she knew,
and her heart had simply craved and yearned over them without the
least hope of possession. And now, they were hers, but the tresses that
should have adorned the coveted adornments were gone.

But she hugged them to her bosom, and at length she was able to 39
look up with dim eyes and a smile and say: "My hair grows so fast,
Jim!"

And then Della leaped up like a little singed cat and cried, "Oh, 40
oh!"

Jim had not yet seen his beautiful present. She held it out to him 41
eagerly upon her open palm. The dull, precious metal seemed to flash
with a reflection of her bright and ardent spirit.

"Isn't it a dandy, Jim? I hunted all over town to find it. You'll 42
have to look at the time a hundred times a day now. Give me your
watch. I want to see how it looks on it."

Instead of obeying, Jim tumbled down on the couch and put his 43
hands under the back of his head and smiled.

"Dell," said he, "let's put our Christmas presents away and keep 44
'em a while. They're too nice to use just at present. I sold the watch to
get the money to buy your combs. And now suppose you put the
chops on."

The magi, as you know, were wise men—wonderfully wise 45
men—who brought gifts to the Babe in the manger. They invented the
art of giving Christmas gifts. Being wise, their gifts were no doubt
wise ones, possibly bearing the privilege of exchange in case of dupli-
cation. And here I have lamely related to you the uneventful chronicle
of two foolish children in a flat who most unwisely sacrificed for each
other the greatest treasures of their house. But in a last word to the
wise of these days let it be said that of all who give gifts these two
were of the wisest. Of all who give and receive gifts, such as they are
the wisest. Everywhere they are the wisest. They are the magi.

Focusing on the Story

1. Describe Jim and Della's apartment and lifestyle.
2. What time of year is it? What holiday is coming up? What is Della's
   problem?
3. How would you describe Jim and Della's marriage?
4. What are the couple's most valued possessions? Why do they sacrifice their most prized possessions to buy each other gifts?

Interpreting and Evaluating

1. Irony is a result that is the opposite of what might be expected.
   What's ironic about Jim and Della's situation?
2. What do Jim and Della have that is more valuable than the most
   expensive gift?
3. In the last paragraph, O. Henry writes that Della and Jim are "two
   foolish children . . . who most unwisely sacrificed for each other the
   greatest treasures of their house." Are Jim and Della foolish?
   Explain.
4. O. Henry says of Jim and Della that "of all who give and receive
   gifts, such as they are the wisest. . . . They are the magi." What does
   O. Henry mean by this statement? How are Jim and Della the wisest? How are they the magi?
5. Some critics have called "The Gift of the Magi" a fable. If it is
   indeed a fable, what is the moral of the story?
6. Are the best gifts necessarily the most expensive? What are some
   "gifts" that are free?

Ideas for Writing and Further Discussion

1. Although O. Henry doesn't describe Della's character directly, the
   reader can infer what kind of person she is through her thoughts and
   actions. Write a paragraph in which you describe Della's character.
   Support each personality trait with details from the story.
2. What are some gifts you like to give? Are they unusual? To whom
   do you like to give gifts? Write a paragraph or two and describe
   gifts you like to give as well as when and to whom you like to give
   gifts. How does giving gifts make you feel?
3. Write a few paragraphs about the kinds of gifts you like to receive
   and when and from whom you like to receive gifts. How do you feel
   when you receive gifts?
4. Write a paragraph or two describing the best "gift" you ever
   received. The gift might be something other than an object.

5. People all over the world exchange gifts on various occasions. Why do people give gifts? Is it just tradition? Does it make them feel good, or do they want something in return? Write an essay in which you explore some reasons why people give each other gifts.
   Suggested *thesis*: two or three such reasons.
   Each *body paragraph* should explore one reason.
6. Perhaps you dislike giving and receiving gifts. Write an essay in which you explore reasons why you dislike giving or receiving (or both) gifts.
   Suggested *thesis*: a few such reasons.
   Each *body paragraph* should explore one reason only.

Guilt
and
Innocence

❖

The Confession

❖

Anton Chekhov

About the Author

Anton Chekhov was born in Russia in 1860. He received a medical degree but never practiced medicine. Instead, he devoted his life to writing, and today he stands out as one of the greatest short story writers of all time.

Something to Think About

How do demands from others affect our judgment? In this story, a thief is caught and confesses his guilt, but is he the only guilty one?

Words to Keep in Mind

elated *(1)* very happy

miserly *(2)* stingy

haughty *(3)* arrogant

trifling *(7)* of little importance

endure *(10)* tolerate; stand

rubles *(10)* Russian money

guzzle *(13)* drink greedily

gorge *(13)* eat greedily

ethical *(16)* moral

It was a cold clear day. I felt as elated as a cab driver who has been   1
given a gold coin by mistake. I wanted to laugh, to cry, to pray. I was
in seventh heaven: I had just been made a cashier! But I was rejoicing
not because I now could get my hands on something—I was not a
thief, and would have destroyed anyone who had told me that in time
I should be one—I was rejoicing over the promotion and the slight
increase in salary, nothing more.

Also I was happy for another reason: on becoming a cashier I   2
suddenly felt as if I were wearing rose-colored glasses. All at once
people appeared to have changed. My word of honor! Everyone
seemed to have improved! The ugly became beautiful, the wicked,
good; the proud became humble, the miserly, generous. It was as if
my eyes had been opened, and I beheld all man's wonderful, until
now unsuspected qualities. "Strange," I said to myself, either something has happened to them, or I have been stupid not to have noticed
these qualities before. How charming everyone is!"

On the day of my promotion, even Z. N. Kazusov changed. He   3
was a member of the board of directors, a haughty, proud man who
always ignored the small fry. He approached me and—what had happened to him?—smiling affectionately, he clapped me on the back.

"You're too young to be so proud, my boy. It's unforgivable!" he   4
said. "Why don't you ever drop in on us? It's shameful of you not to
visit. The young people generally gather at our house, and it's always
festive there. My daughters are forever asking me: 'Why don't you
invite Gregory Kuzmich, Papa? He's so nice!' But is it possible to get
him to come? Well, in any case, I'll try, I told them. I'll ask him. Now,
don't give yourself airs, my boy, do come."

Amazing! What had happened to Mr. Kazusov? Had he gone out   5
of his mind? He had always been a regular ogre, and now look at him!

On returning home that same day I was astounded: Mama served   6
not the usual two courses at dinner, but four! For tea in the evening
there was jam and white bread. The following day, again four courses,
again jam; and when guests dropped in, we drank chocolate. The third
day it was the same.

From *Anton Chekhov: Selected Stories* by Anton Chekhov. © 1960 by Ann Dunnigan.
By permission of Dutton Signet, a division of Penguin Putnam, Inc.

"Mama," I said, "what's the matter with you? Why this burst of 7
generosity? You know, my salary wasn't doubled. The increase was
trifling."

Mama looked at me in surprise. "Humph! What do you expect to 8
do with the money—save it?"

God only knows what got into them. Papa ordered a fur coat, 9
bought a new cap, took a relaxing vacation, and began to eat grapes—
in winter!

Within a few days I received a letter from my brother. This 10
brother could not endure me. We had parted over a difference of opinion: he considered me a selfish parasite, incapable of self-sacrifice,
and for this he despised me. In his letter he now wrote: "Dear brother,
I love you, and you cannot imagine what hellish torture our quarrel
has caused me. Let us make it up. Let us each extend a hand to the
other, and may peace triumph! I beg you! Awaiting your reply, I
embrace you and remain your most loving and affectionate brother,
Yevlampy." Oh, my dear brother! I answered him saying that I
embraced him and rejoiced. Within a week I received a telegram:
"Thanks. Happy. Send hundred rubles. Most urgent. Embrace you.
Yevlampy." I sent the hundred rubles.

Even she changed. She did not love me. Once when I had made so 11
bold as to hint that I admired her, she laughed in my face. On meeting
me a week after my promotion, however, she dimpled, smiled, and
looked flustered. "What's happened to you?" she asked, gazing at me.
"You've grown so handsome. When did you manage to do that?" And
then, "Let's dance. . . ."

Sweetheart! Within a month she had given me a mother-in-law. I 12
had become that handsome! When money was needed for the wedding
I took three hundred rubles out of the cash box. Why not take it, when
you know you are going to put it back as soon as you receive your
raise? At the same time I took out a hundred rubles for Kazusov. He
had asked for a loan and it was impossible to refuse him; he was a big
wheel in the office and could have anyone fired at a moment's notice.

A week before the arrest it was suggested that I give a party. What 13
the devil, let them guzzle and gorge, if that's what they want! I did not
count the guests that evening, but I recall that all eight of my rooms
were swarming with people, young and old. There were those before
whom even Kazusov had to show humility.

His daughters—the oldest being my treasure—were in dazzling 14 attire. The flowers alone with which they covered themselves cost me over a thousand rubles. It was very festive, with glittering chandeliers, deafening music, and plenty of champagne. There were long speeches and short toasts; one journalist presented me with a poem, another with a song. "We in Russia do not know how to appreciate such men as Gregory Kuzmich," cried Kazusov. "It's a shame! Russia is to be pitied!"

All those who were shouting, applauding and kissing me, were 15 whispering behind my back, thumbing their noses at me. I saw their smiles and heard their sighs. "He stole it, the crook!" they whispered, with evil grins. But their sighing and smirking did not prevent them from eating, drinking, and enjoying themselves. Wolves never ate as they did.

My wife, flashing gold and diamonds, came up to me and whis- 16 pered: "They are saying that you stole the money. If it's true, I warn you, I cannot go on living with a thief. I'll leave!" And she smoothed down her five-thousand ruble gown. The devil take them all! That very evening Kazusov had five thousand from me. Yevlampy took an equal amount. "If what they are whispering about you is true," said my ethical brother, as he pocketed the money, "watch out! I will not be brother to a thief!"

After the party I drove them all to the country in a sleigh. We fin- 17 ished up at six in the morning. Exhausted, they lay back in the sleigh, and, as they started off for home, cried out in farewell: "Inspection tomorrow! Thanks."

My dear ladies and gentlemen, I got caught; or, to state it more 18 fully: yesterday I was respected and honored on all sides. Today I am a scoundrel and a thief. . . . Cry out, now, accuse me, spread the news, judge and wonder. Banish me, write editorials and throw stones, only, please—not everyone, not everyone!

Focusing on the Story

1. Who is the narrator (the character who tells the story), and what pronoun is used throughout to identify him?
2. Where is the narrator when he is making his confession?

3. On becoming cashier, Gregory Kuzmich feels "as if [he] were wearing rose-colored glasses" and says that "people appeared to have changed." How have the people changed? What causes the change? Is the change temporary or permanent?
4. Why does Gregory Kuzmich continue to shower people with more and more money? What do they give him in return?
5. What are the people whispering behind Gregory Kuzmich's back? What are they threatening to do if they find out that Gregory Kuzmich is guilty of stealing?

Interpreting and Evaluating

1. Why does author Anton Chekhov reveal the arrest so early in the story? How would the story be different if told in chronological order or in the order the events happened?
2. Is the narrator the only guilty one? Do his so-called friends know that the money is not his to give away? Explain.
3. The narrator is unable to grasp that his family and "friends" are taking advantage of him. As readers, however, we soon catch on. Why has Chekhov created such a naive narrator? What is the effect of such a naive narrator on the story as a whole?
4. What common human weaknesses does Chekhov expose and mock in this story?
5. Rather than telling his story in an objective way, Gregory Kuzmich uses subjective words and phrases in order to win the reader's understanding and approval. Point out several such biased or slanted words. Do you feel sympathy toward Gregory Kuzmich? Why or why not?

Ideas for Writing and Further Discussion

1. Most people want to "fit in" and try to do what is expected by the group. Think about your group of friends and peers. Write a narrative composition describing a time when you decided to go along with the group, even though it was against your better judgment. Was the result favorable or disastrous? What did you learn from the experience? (If you don't want to write about yourself, write about someone you know.)

2. Write about a time when you dared stand alone and go against the group because you didn't want to compromise your integrity. Describe what happened. Were you rewarded for your courage? What did you learn from your experience? It's not necessary to write a formal thesis statement in a narrative essay, but you may wish to start with a general statement that expresses an attitude toward the experience.
3. Peer pressure is not always bad, of course. Write an essay in which you discuss how peer pressure can be both good and bad. To prove your point, use examples from your own life when you or someone you know yielded to peer pressure, or use examples from the story. Suggested *thesis*: three or four ways peer pressure can be both good and bad.

   Each *body paragraph* may develop one such way. (Make one list of how peer pressure can be good and another list of how peer pressure can be bad. Use these lists to organize your body paragraphs.)

Han's Crime

❖

Shiga Naoya

About the Author

Shiga Naoya (Shiga is his last name or family name) was born in Japan in 1883 and is best known for his short stories. In most of his stories, the emphasis is less on what happens and more on how the characters feel. The Japanese refer to his genre as "state-of-mind" fiction. Shiga Naoya died in 1971.

Something to Think About

A Chinese juggler and knife-thrower named Han kills his wife during a performance in front of a large audience by driving a knife through her neck. But is this incident an act of premeditated murder and thus perhaps an example of a perfect crime, or is it an accident?

Words to Keep in Mind

carotid artery *(1)* main artery that carries blood from the heart to the head

interrogating *(4)* questioning

perplexed *(13)* puzzled

solicitation *(17)* request to do something

disposition *(18)* temperament; personality

detriment *(19)* injury; damage

profligacy *(23)* careless spending; wastefulness

demeanor *(36)* behavior

discord *(44)* disagreement

assertive *(77)* bold; aggressive

grub *(97)* wormlike larva of an insect

alleviate *(105)* make easier to endure; lessen

premonition *(105)* forewarning

conjecture *(117)* guess

plea *(117)* excuse; defense

plausible *(117)* reasonable

In an unusual incident, a young Chinese juggler called Han severed 1
his wife's carotid artery during a performance with a knife the size of
a carver. The young wife died on the spot. Han was immediately
arrested.

The act was witnessed by the owner-manager of the troupe, a 2
Chinese stagehand, the introducer, and an audience of over three hundred. A policeman, sitting on a chair set up slightly above and at the
edge of the audience, also saw it. But it was not at all known whether
this incident, which had occurred before so many eyes, was a deliberate act or an accident.

For this performance, Han made his wife stand in front of a thick 3
board the size of a rain shutter. From a distance of twelve feet, he
hurled several of the carver-sized knives, each with a shout, to form
an outline of her body not two inches removed from it.

The judge commenced by interrogating the owner-manager. 4

"Is that performance a particularly difficult one?" 5

"No. For an experienced performer, it is not that difficult. All 6
that's required is an alert, healthy state of mind."

"If that's so, an incident like this should not have happened even 7
as a mistake."

"Of course, unless one is sure of the performer—extremely 8
sure—one cannot allow the performance."

From *The Paper Door and Other Stories* by Shiga Naoya. (Shiga is the last name.)
English translation used by permission of Lane Dunlop. Columbia University Press,
2001. Reprinted by permission of the publisher.

"Well, then. Do you think it was a deliberate act?"   9

"No. I don't. The performance requires experience, instinctive   10
skill and nothing else. But one cannot say that it will always come off
with a machinelike precision. It's a fact that we never thought something like this would happen. But I do not think it is fair, now that it
has happened, to say that we had considered the possibility and hold
it against us."

"Well, what do you think it was?"   11

"I don't know."   12

The judge was perplexed. There was, here, the fact of homicide.   13
But there was absolutely no proof as to whether it was premeditated
murder or manslaughter (if the former, the judge thought, there was
never such a cunning murder as this). Next calling in the Chinese
stagehand, who had served with the troupe longer than Han, the judge
questioned him.

"What is Han's ordinary behavior like?"   14

"He's a good person. He doesn't gamble, fool around with other   15
women, or drink. About a year ago, he converted to Christianity. His
English is good, and when he has the time he often reads collections
of sermons."

"And his wife?"   16

"She was a good person too. As you know, people of our sort   17
aren't always known for their strict morals. One often hears of somebody running off with somebody else's wife. Han's wife was a beautiful woman, although on the small side, and she now and then got
solicitations of that sort. But she never took up with such people."

"What were their dispositions like?"   18

"Toward others, they were both extremely kind and gentle. They   19
never thought of themselves and never got angry. And yet" (here the
stagehand paused. Thinking a moment, he went on) "I'm afraid this
may be to Han's detriment, but to tell the truth, strangely enough,
those two, who were so kind, gentle, and self-effacing with others,
when it came to their own relationship, were surprisingly cruel to
each other."

"Why was that?"   20

"I don't know why."   21

"Had they always been that way?"   22

"No. About two years ago, the wife gave birth. The baby was pre-   23
mature, and died in three days or so. But after that, it was clear even
to us that their relationship was slowly going to the bad. They would
often have arguments over the most trivial things. At such times, Han
would suddenly turn dead pale. But in the end, no matter what, he
always fell silent. He never mistreated his wife. Of course, that's most
likely because his religion forbade him to. But sometimes, when you
looked at his face, there was a terrible, uncontrollable anger in it.
Once, I suggested that if things were so bad between them it might be
good to get a divorce. But Han said that even if his wife had reasons
for seeking a divorce, he himself had none. Han followed his own
will in the matter. He even said that there was no way he could love
his wife. It was only natural, he said, if a woman he did not love gradually came not to love him. It was why he took to reading the Bible
and collections of sermons. He seemed to think that by somehow
calming his heart he could correct his fairly unruly feelings of hatred.
After all, he had no reason to hate his wife. She, too, deserved sympathy. After their marriage, they had travelled about as road-players for
nearly three years. Owing to an older brother's profligacy, the family
back home was already broken up and gone. Even if she had left Han
and gone back, nobody would have trusted a woman who'd been on
the road four years enough to marry her. Bad as things were, she had
no choice but to stay with Han."

"What is *your* opinion of the incident?"   24

"You mean whether it was deliberate or an accident?"   25

"Yes."   26

"Actually, I've thought a lot about that. But the more I've   27
thought, the more I've come, by degrees, not to understand anything."

"Why is that?"   28

"I don't know why. I really do not. I think anyone would have the   29
same problem. I asked the introducer what he thought, but he said he
didn't know either."

"Well, at the instant it happened, what did you think?"   30

"I thought: He's murdered her. I did think that."   31

"Is that so?"   32

"But the introducer told me that he thought: He's bungled it."   33

"Is that so? But isn't that what he would think, not knowing too   34
much about their relationship?"

"Maybe so. But later, I thought that my thinking he'd murdered   35
her might also, in the same way, simply have been because I knew a
good deal about their relationship."

"What was Han's demeanor just then?"   36

"He gave a short cry: 'Aa!' That was what drew my attention to   37
what had happened. The blood suddenly gushed out of the wife's
neck. Even so, she remained upright for a moment. Her body was held
in place by the knife's sticking in the board behind her. Then, all of a
sudden, her knees buckled, the knife came out and collapsing all
together she fell forward. There was nothing anyone could do. We all
of us just went stiff and watched. But I can't be sure of anything. I
didn't have the leisure to observe Han's demeanor just then. But it
seems to me that for those few seconds he was just like us. It was only
afterward that I thought: He's murdered her at last. Han went dead
pale and stood there with his eyes closed. We drew the curtain down
and tried to revive the woman, but she was already dead. Han, his face
bluish with excitement, blurted out: 'How could I make such a blun-
der?' Then he knelt, in a long silent prayer."

"Was his demeanor agitated then?"   38

"It was somewhat agitated."   39

"Good. If I have any further questions, I'll call you."   40

Dismissing the Chinese stagehand, the judge finally had Han   41
himself brought in. Han, his face drawn and pale, was an intelligent-
looking man. It was clear at a glance to the judge that he was suffer-
ing from nervous exhaustion. As soon as Han had seated himself, the
judge said: "I've been questioning the owner-manager and the stagehand. I will now ask you some questions." Han nodded.

"Have you never loved your wife at all?"   42

"From the day I married her until the day she had the baby, I   43
loved my wife with all my heart."

"Why did the birth become a source of discord?"   44

"Because I knew it wasn't my child."   45

"Do you know who the father was?"   46

"I have an idea it was my wife's cousin."   47

"Did you know the man?"   48

"He was a close friend of mine. It was he who suggested that we   49
get married. He introduced me to her."

"Was there a relationship before she married you?"   50

"Of course there was. The baby was born the eighth month after   51
the marriage."

"The stagehand said it was a premature birth."   52

"That's because I told him it was."   53

"The baby died shortly afterwards?"   54

"Yes."   55

"What was the cause of death?"   56

"It choked at the breast."   57

"Was that a deliberate act of your wife's?"   58

"She said it was an accident."   59

The judge, falling silent, looked intently at Han. Han, eyes low-   60
ered in his raised face, waited for the next question.

"Did your wife tell you about the relationship?"   61

"No, she didn't. Nor did I ask her about it. I felt that the baby's   62
death was a judgement on her for what she'd done. I thought that I
myself should be as forgiving as possible."

"But, in the end, you couldn't forgive her?"   63

"That's right. My feeling remained that the baby's death wasn't   64
enough of a judgement. At times, when I thought about it by myself, I
could be rather forgiving. But then, my wife would come in. She
would go about her business. As I looked at her, at her body, I could
not keep down my displeasure."

"You didn't think of divorcing her?"   65

"I often thought I'd like a divorce. But I never said anything."   66

"Why was that?"   67

"I was weak. And my wife had said that if I divorced her she   68
would not survive."

"Did your wife love you?"   69

"She did not love me."   70

"If that was so, why did she say such a thing?"   71

"I think it was from the necessity of going on living. Her brother   72
had broken up the household back home, and she knew that no
respectable man would marry a woman who'd been the wife of a
road-player. And her feet were too small for ordinary work."

"What were your sexual relations?"   73

"I believe they were probably not much different from those of an   74
average couple."

"Did your wife feel any sympathy for you?"   75

"I can't think she felt any sympathy. I believe that for my wife 76
living with me was an extraordinary hardship. But the patience with
which she endured hardship was beyond what one would have
thought possible even for a man. My wife simply observed, with cruel
eyes, the gradual destruction of my life. My writhing, desperate
attempts to save myself, to enter upon my true life, she coolly, from
the side and without the slightest wish to help, as if surrounding me,
looked on at."

"Why were you unable to take a more assertive, resolute atti- 77
tude?"

"Because I was thinking about various things." 78

"Various things? What sort of things?" 79

"I thought I would act in such a way as to leave no room for error. 80
But, in the end, those thoughts never offered any solution."

"Did you ever think of killing your wife?" 81

Han did not answer. The judge repeated his question. Even then, 82
Han did not answer immediately. Then, he said:

"I'd often thought, before then, that it would be good if she were 83
dead."

"Then, if the law had allowed it, you might have killed her?" 84

"I was afraid of the law, and I had never had such thoughts 85
before. It was merely because I was weak. But even though I was
weak, my desire to live my own life was strong."

"So, after that, you thought about killing your wife?" 86

"I didn't make my mind up to do it. But I did think about it." 87

"How long before the incident was this?" 88

"The night before. Toward daybreak." 89

"Had you quarrelled that evening?" 90

"Yes." 91

"What about?" 92

"Something so trivial it isn't worth mentioning." 93

"Tell me anyway." 94

"It was about food. When I'm hungry, I get irritable. The way she 95
dawdled over the preparations for supper made me angry."

"Did you quarrel more violently than usual?" 96

"No. But I remained excited longer than usual. It was because 97
lately I'd felt intolerably frustrated by the fact that I did not have a
life of my own. I went to bed, but I couldn't sleep at all. I thought

about all sorts of things. I felt as if my present existence in which, like a grub suspended in midair, I looked to one side and the other, always hesitating, without the courage to want what I wanted, without the courage to get rid of what was unbearable, was all due to my relationship with my wife. I could see no light in my future. A desire to seek the light was burning inside me. Or, if it was not, it was trying to catch fire. But my relationship with my wife would not let it. The flame was not out. It was smouldering, in a fitful, ugly way. What with the pain and unhappiness of it all, I was being poisoned. When the poisoning was complete, I would die. Although alive, I would be a dead man. And though this was what I had come to, I was still trying to put up with it. It would be good if she died—one part of me kept having that dirty, hateful thought. If this was how things were, why didn't I kill her? The consequences of such an act did not trouble me now. I might be put in jail. Who could tell how much better life in jail might be than this life? I would cross that bridge when I came to it. It would be enough if, in any way I could, I broke through whatever came up at the time it came up. Even if I broke through, and broke through, I might not break through all the way. But if I went on breaking through until the day I died, that would be my true life. I almost forgot that my wife was lying beside me. At last, I grew tired. But even though I was tired, it was not the sort of fatigue that leads to sleep. My thoughts began to blur. As my tensed up feelings relaxed, my dark thoughts of murder faded away. A feeling of loneliness came over me, as after a nightmare. I even felt pity for my own weak spirit, that the ability to think hard had, in a single night, become so feeble and forlorn. And then, at last, the night was over. It seemed to me that my wife hadn't slept either."

"When you got up, was everything as usual between you?"   98

"Neither of us said a word to each other."   99

"Why didn't you think of leaving your wife?"   100

"Do you mean that as a desired result, it would have come to the   101
same thing?"

"Yes."   102

"For me, there was a great difference."   103

Saying this, Han looked at the judge and was silent. The judge,   104
his face softening, nodded.

"But, between my thinking about such a thing and actually deciding to kill her, there was still a wide gap. That day, from early morning on, I felt insanely keyed up. Because of my bodily fatigue, my
nerves were edgy, without elasticity. Unable to remain still, I stayed
outside all morning. I walked about restlessly, away from the others. I
kept thinking that no matter what I would have to do something. But I
no longer thought of killing her, as I had the night before. And I was
not at all worried about that day's performance. If I had been, I would
not have chosen that particular act. We had many other acts. Finally,
that evening, our turn came. Then also, I was not thinking of such a
thing. As usual, I demonstrated to the audience that the knives were
sharp by slicing through a piece of paper and sticking a knife into the
stage. My wife, heavily made up and wearing a gaudy Chinese costume, came on. Her stage manner was no different than always.
Greeting the audience with a winsome smile, she stepped up to the
thick board and stood bolt upright with her back to it. A knife in my
hand, I stood at a set distance straight across from her. For the first
time since the night before, we exchanged looks. Only then did I realize the danger of having chosen this act for tonight. Unless I practiced
the utmost care, I thought, there would be trouble. I must alleviate, as
best I could, the day's restless agitation and my strained, edgy nerves.
But no matter how I tried, a weariness that had eaten into my heart
would not let me. I began to feel that I could not trust my own arm.
Closing my eyes, I attempted to calm myself. My body started to
sway. The moment came. I drove in the first knife above her head. It
went in slightly higher than usual. Then I drove in one knife each
under the pits of her arms which were raised to shoulder level. As
each knife left my fingertips, something clung to it an instant, as if to
hold it back. I felt as if I no longer knew where the knives would go
in. Each time one hit, I thought: Thank God. Calm down, calm down,
I thought. But I could feel in my arm the constraint that comes from a
thing's having become conscious. I drove in a knife to the left of her
throat. I was about to drive in the next one to the right, when suddenly
a strange look came over her face. She must have felt an impulse of
violent fear. Did she have a premonition that the knife about to fly at
her would go through her neck? I don't know. I only felt that face of
violent fear, thrown back at my heart with the same force as the knife.

Dizziness struck me. But even so, with all my strength, almost without a target, as though aiming in the dark, I threw the knife . . .”

The judge was silent.   106

“I’ve killed her at last, I thought.”   107

“How do you mean? That you’d done it on purpose?”   108

“Yes. I suddenly felt as if I had.”   109

“Afterwards, you knelt by the body in silent prayer . . . ?”   110

“That was a trick that occurred to me at the moment. I knew   111
everyone thought I seriously believed in Christianity. While pretend-
ing to pray, I was thinking about what attitude I should take.”

“You felt sure that what you’d done was intentional?”   112

“Yes. And I thought right away I could make out it was an acci-   113
dent.”

“But why did you think it was deliberate murder?”   114

“Because of my feelings, which were unhinged.”   115

“So you thought you’d skillfully deceived the others?”   116

“Thinking about it later, I was shocked at myself. I acted sur-   117
prised in a natural manner, was considerably agitated, and also dis-
played grief. But any perceptive person, I believe, could have seen
that I was playacting. Recalling my behavior, I sweated cold sweat.
That night, I decided that I would have to be found innocent. First of
all, I was extremely encouraged by the fact that there was not a scrap
of objective proof of my crime. Everyone knew we’d been on bad
terms, of course, so there was bound to be a suspicion of murder. I
couldn’t do anything about that. But if I insisted, throughout, that it
was an accident, that would be the end of it. That we’d gotten along
badly might make people conjecture, but it was no proof. In the end, I
thought, I would be acquitted for lack of evidence. Thinking back
over the incident, I made up a rough version of my plea, as plausible
as possible, so that it would seem like an accident. Soon, though, for
some reason, a doubt rose up in me as to whether I myself believed it
was murder. The night before, I had thought about killing her, but was
that alone a reason for deciding, myself, that it was murder?
Gradually, despite myself, I became unsure. A sudden excitement
swept over me. I felt so excited I couldn’t sit still. I was so happy, I
was beside myself. I wanted to shout for joy.”

“Was it because you yourself could now believe that it was an   118
accident?”

"No. I'm still unsure of that. It was because it was completely 119
unclear, even to myself, which it had been. It was because I could
now tell the truth and be found innocent. Being found innocent meant
everything to me now. For that purpose, rather than trying to deceive
myself and insisting that it was an accident, it was far better to be able
to be honest, even if it meant saying I didn't know which it was. I
could no longer assert that it was an accident, nor, on the other hand,
could I say that it was a deliberate act. I was so happy because come
what may it was no longer a question of a confession of guilt."

Han fell silent. The judge, also, was silent for a moment. Then, as 120
if to himself, he said: "On the whole, it seems to be the truth." And
then: "By the way, do you not feel the slightest sorrow about your
wife's death?"

"None whatsoever. And up to now, no matter what my feelings of 121
hatred for her, I never imagined that I'd be able to talk so cheerfully
about her death."

"That will be all. You may step down," the judge said. Han, after 122
a slight wordless bow, left the room.

The judge felt an excitement, he could not put a name to it, surge 123
up in him.

Quickly, he took up his pen. And, then and there, he wrote: 124
"Innocent."

Focusing on the Story

1. Describe the relationship between Han and his wife. What caused
   their relationship to deteriorate?
2. Soon after their marriage, Han's wife had a baby. How did Han feel
   about the baby? Why did he feel the way he did? What happened to
   the baby?
3. How does the stagehand describe Han and his wife? How do the
   owner-manager and the stagehand think the incident happened?
4. How had Han spent the night before the performance? How did he
   spend the morning of the performance? How did he feel immediately before and after his wife's death?
5. How does Han himself explain the incident? Why does he change
   his mind?

Interpreting and Evaluating

1. The first few paragraphs of the story sound like a newspaper account. What effect does such an objective tone have on the story? Instead of focusing on the plot, what does the author want the reader to focus on?
2. Why does the author make a point of the fact that Han had converted to Christianity and that he read collections of sermons?
3. The story is written by a Japanese writer for a Japanese audience, yet the main character is Chinese. What might be a reason for making Han a different nationality?
4. The reader is given clues of both guilt and innocence along the way. If this had been a trial by jury and you had been on that jury, what would your verdict have been? Give reasons for your answer.
5. What do you think Han's life will be like after this incident?
6. Is there such a thing as a perfect crime? Explain your answer.

Ideas for Writing and Further Discussion

1. The title of the story is "Han's Crime." If Han in fact committed a crime, what was his crime? Write a paragraph in which you explore the answer to this question.
2. Write a paragraph in which you defend Han's action. Look for evidence in the story that points to Han's innocence.
3. Take the opposite stand and argue against Han's innocence. Point to evidence in the story that shows that Han is guilty of murder and should be punished.
4. Try to seriously observe an ordinary situation around you. You may, for example, observe a child playing in a park or on the beach, or you may observe an argument between your neighbors or a dispute between a store clerk and a customer. Try to imagine how the people feel. Write a short story of your own in which you focus on how the people feel.

Horse Thief

❖

Erskine Caldwell

About the Author

Erskine Caldwell, an American novelist and short story writer, was born in 1903. He spent much of his youth traveling through the South, and most of his works depict the harsh reality of the rural South. *God's Little Acre* and *Tobacco Road* are his best-known novels.

Something to Think About

How can a small mischief, an innocent lie, lead to serious trouble?

Words to Keep in Mind

calico *(1)* spotted

bridle *(3)* head gear for controlling a horse

shy *(13)* jump or move suddenly from being startled

pommel *(13)* post on the front of a Western saddle

halter *(13)* leather or rope headband used for tying a horse

hitched *(14)* tied the horse

I didn't steal Lud Moseley's calico horse.   1

From *Vanity Fair,* November 1933. © 1933 by Conde Nast Publications, Inc.
© renewed 1960 by Erskine Caldwell.

People all over have been trying to make me out a thief, but any- 2
body who knows me at all will tell you that I've never been in trouble
like this before in all my life. Mr. John Turner will tell you all about
me. I've worked for him, off and on, for I don't know exactly how
many years. I reckon I've worked for him just about all my life, since
I was a boy. Mr. John knows I wouldn't steal a horse. That's why I say
I didn't steal Lud Moseley's, like he swore I did. I didn't grow up just
to turn out to be a horse thief.

Night before last, Mr. John told me to ride his mare, Betsy. I said 3
I wanted to go off a little way after something, and he told me to go
ahead and ride Betsy, like I have been doing every Sunday night for
going on two years now. Mr. John told me to take the Texas saddle,
but I told him I didn't care about riding saddle. I like to ride with a
bridle and reins, and nothing else. That's the best way to ride, anyway. And where I was going I didn't want to have a squeaking saddle
under me. I wasn't up to no mischief. It was just a little private business of my own that nobody has got a right to call me down about. I
nearly always rode saddle Sunday nights, but night before last was
Thursday night, and that's why I didn't have a saddle when I went.

Mr. John Turner will tell you I'm not the kind to go off and get 4
into trouble. Ask Mr. John about me. He has known me all my life,
and I've never given him or anybody else trouble.

When I took Betsy out of the stable that night after supper, Mr. 5
John came out to the barnyard and asked me over again if I didn't
want to take the Texas saddle. That mare, Betsy, is a little rawboned,
but I didn't mind that. I told Mr. John I'd just as lief ride bareback. He
said it was all right with him if I wanted to get sawn in two, and to go
ahead and do like I pleased about it. He was standing right there all
the time, rubbing Betsy's mane, and trying to find out where I was
going, without coming right out and asking me. But he knew all the
time where I was going, because he knows all about me. I reckon he
just wanted to have a laugh at me, but he couldn't do that if I didn't let
on where I was headed. So he told me it was all right to ride his mare
without a saddle if I didn't want to be bothered with one, and I opened
the gate and rode off down the road toward Bishop's crossroads.

That was night before last—Thursday night. It was a little after 6
dark then, but I could see Mr. John standing at the barnyard gate,

leaning on it a little, and watching me ride off. I'd been plowing that day, over in the new ground, and I was dog-tired. That's one reason why I didn't gallop off like I always did on Sunday nights. I rode away slow, letting Betsy take her own good time, because I wasn't in such a big hurry, after all. I had about two hours' time to kill, and only a little over three miles to go. That's why I went off like that.

Everybody knows I've been going to see Lud Moseley's youngest 7 daughter, Naomi. I was going to see her that night. But I couldn't show up there till about nine thirty. Lud Moseley wouldn't let me come to see her but once a week, on Sunday nights, and night before last was Thursday. I'd been there to see her three or four times before on Thursday nights that Lud Moseley didn't know about. Naomi told me to come to see her on Thursday nights. That's why I had been going there when Lud Moseley said I couldn't come to his house but once a week. Naomi told me to come anyway, and she had been coming out to the swing under the trees in the front yard to meet me.

I haven't got a thing in the world against Lud Moseley. Mr. John 8 Turner will tell you I haven't. I don't especially like him, but that's to be expected, and he knows why. Once a week isn't enough to go to see a girl you like a lot, like I do Naomi. And I reckon she likes me a little, or she wouldn't tell me to come to see her on Thursday nights, when Lud Moseley told me not to come. Lud Moseley thinks if I go to see her more than once a week that maybe we'll take it into our heads to go get married without giving him a chance to catch on. That's why he said I couldn't come to his house but once a week, on Sunday nights.

He's fixing to have me sent to the penitentiary for twenty years 9 for stealing his calico horse, Lightfoot. I reckon he knows good and well I didn't steal the horse, but he figures he's got a chance to put me out of the way till he can get Naomi married to somebody else. That's the way I figure it all out, because everybody in this part of the country who ever heard tell of me knows I'm not a horse thief. Mr. John Turner will tell you that about me. Mr. John knows me better than that. I've worked for him so long he even tried once to make me out as one of the family, but I wouldn't let him do that.

So, night before last, Thursday night, I rode off from home bare- 10 back, on Betsy. I killed a little time down at the creek, about a mile down the road from where we live, and when I looked at my watch again, it was nine o'clock sharp. I got on Betsy and rode off toward Lud Moseley's place. Everything was still and quiet around the house and barn. It was just about Lud's bedtime then. I rode right up to the barnyard gate, like I always did on Thursday nights. I could see a light up in Naomi's room, where she slept with her older sister, Mary Lee. We had always figured on Mary Lee's being out with somebody else, or maybe being ready to go to sleep by nine thirty. When I looked up at their window, I could see Naomi lying across her bed, and Mary Lee was standing beside the bed talking to her about something. That looked bad, because when Mary Lee tried to make Naomi undress and go to bed before she did, it always meant that it would take Naomi another hour or more to get out of the room, because she had to wait for Mary Lee to go to sleep before she could leave. She had to wait for Mary Lee to go to sleep, and then she had to get up and dress in the dark before she could come down to the front yard and meet me in the swing under the trees.

I sat there on Betsy for ten or fifteen minutes, waiting to see how Naomi was going to come out with her sister. I reckon if we had let Mary Lee in on the secret she would have behaved all right about it, but on some account or other Naomi couldn't make up her mind to run the risk of it. There was a mighty chance that she would have misbehaved about it and gone straight and told Lud Moseley, and we didn't want to run that risk.

After a while I saw Naomi get up and start to undress. I knew right away that that meant waiting another hour or longer for her to be able to come and meet me. The moon was starting to rise, and it was getting to be as bright as day out there in the barnyard. I'd been in the habit of opening the gate and turning Betsy loose in the yard, but I was scared to do it night before last. If Lud Moseley should get up for a drink of water or something, and happen to look out toward the barn and see a horse standing there, he would either think it was one of his and come out and lock it in the stalls, or else he would catch on it was me out there. Anyway, as soon as he saw Betsy, he would have known it wasn't his mare, and there would have been the mischief to pay right there and then. So I opened the barn door and led Betsy inside and put her in the first empty stall I could find in the dark. I was scared to strike a light, because I didn't know but what Lud Moseley would be looking out the window just at that time and see the flare of the match. I put Betsy in the stall, closed the door, and came back outside to wait for Naomi to find a chance to come out and meet me in the swing in the yard.

It was about twelve thirty or one o'clock when I got ready to leave   13 for home. The moon had been clouded, and it was darker than everything in the barn. I couldn't see my hand in front of me, it was that dark. I was scared to strike a light that time, too, and I felt my way in and opened the stall door and stepped inside to lead Betsy out. I couldn't see a thing, and when I found her neck, I thought she must have slipped her bridle like she was always doing when she had to stand too long to suit her. I was afraid to ride her home without a lead of some kind, because I was scared she might shy in the barnyard and start tearing around out there and wake up Lud Moseley. I felt around on the ground for the bridle, but I couldn't find it anywhere. Then I went back to the stall door and felt on it, thinking I might have taken it off myself when I was all excited at the start, and there was a halter hanging up. I slipped it over her head and led her out. It was still so dark I couldn't see a thing, and I had to feel my way outside and through the barnyard gate. When I got to the road, I threw a leg over her, and started for home without wasting any more time around Lud Moseley's place. I thought she trotted a little funny, because she had a swaying swing that made me slide from side to side, and I didn't have a saddle pommel to hold on to. I was all wrought up about getting away from there without getting caught up with, and I didn't think a thing about it. But I got home all right and slipped the halter off and put her in her stall. It was around one or two o'clock in the morning then.

The next morning after breakfast, when I was getting ready to   14 catch the mules and gear them up to start plowing in the new ground again, Lud Moseley and three or four other men, including the sheriff, came riding lickety-split up the road from town and hitched at the rack. Mr. John came out and slapped the sheriff on the back and told him a funny story. They carried on like that for nearly half an hour, and then the sheriff asked Mr. John where I was. Mr. John told him I was getting ready to go off to the new ground, where we had planted a crop of corn that spring, and then the sheriff said he had a warrant for me. Mr. John

asked him what for, a joke or something? And the sheriff told him it
was for stealing Lud Moseley's calico horse, Lightfoot. Mr. John
laughed at him, because he still thought it just a joke, but the sheriff
pulled out the paper and showed it to him. Mr. John still wouldn't
believe it, and he told them there was a mix-up somewhere, because,
he told them, I wouldn't steal a horse. Mr. John knows I'm not a horse
thief. I've never been in any kind of trouble before in all my life.

They brought me to town right away and put me in the cell room   15
at the sheriff's jail. I knew I hadn't stole Lud Moseley's horse, and I
wasn't scared a bit about it. But right after they brought me to town,
they all rode back and the sheriff looked in the barn and found Lud
Moseley's calico horse, Lightfoot, in Betsy's stall. Mr. John said
things were all mixed up, because he knew I didn't steal the horse,
and he knew I wouldn't do it. But the horse was there, the calico one,
Lightfoot, and his halter was hanging on the stall door. After that they
went back to Lud Moseley's and measured my foot tracks in the barnyard, and then they found Betsy's bridle. Lud Moseley said I had rode
Mr. John's mare over there, turned her loose, and put the bridle on his
Lightfoot and rode off. They never did say how come the halter got to
Mr. John's stable, then. Lud Moseley's stall door was not locked, and
it wasn't broken down. It looks now like I forgot to shut it tight when
I put Betsy in, because she got out someway and came home of her
own accord sometime that night.

Lud Moseley says he's going to send me away for twenty years,   16
where I won't have a chance to worry him over his youngest daughter, Naomi. He wants her to marry a widowed farmer over beyond
Bishop's crossroads who runs twenty plows and who's got a big white
house with fifteen rooms in it. Mr. John Turner says he'll hire the best
lawyer in town to take up my case, but it don't look like it will do
much good, because my footprints are all over Lud Moseley's barnyard, and his Lightfoot was in Mr. John's stable.

I reckon I could worm out of it someway, if I made up my mind to   17
do it. But I don't like to do things like that. It would put Naomi in a
bad way, because if I said I was there seeing her, and had put Betsy in
the stall to keep her quiet, and took Lightfoot out by mistake in the
dark when I got ready to leave—well, it would just look bad, that's
all. She would have to say she was in the habit of slipping out of the
house to see me after everybody had gone to sleep, on Thursday

nights, and it would just look bad all around. She might take it into her head someday that she'd rather marry somebody else than me, and by that time she'd have a bad name for having been mixed up with me—and slipping out of the house to meet me after bedtime.

Naomi knows I'm no horse thief. She knows how it all hap-   18
pened—that I rode Lud Moseley's calico horse, Lightfoot, off by mistake in the dark, and left the stall door unfastened, and Betsy got out and came home of her own accord.

Lud Moseley has been telling people all around the courthouse as   19
how he is going to send me away for twenty years so he can get Naomi married to that widowed farmer who runs twenty plows. Lud Moseley is right proud of it, it looks like to me, because he's got me cornered in a trap, and maybe he will get me sent away sure enough before Naomi gets a chance to tell what she knows is true.

But, somehow, I don't know if she'll say it if she does get the   20
chance. Everybody knows I'm nothing but a hired man at Mr. John Turner's, and I've been thinking that maybe Naomi might not come right out and tell what she knows, after all.

I'd come right out and explain to the sheriff how the mix-up hap-   21
pened, but I sort of hate to mention Naomi's name in the mess. If it had been a Sunday night, instead of night before last, a Thursday, I could—well, it would just sound too bad, that's all.

If Naomi comes to town and tells what she knows, I won't say a   22
word to stop her, because that'll mean she's willing to say it and marry me.

But if she stays at home, and lets Lud Moseley and that widowed   23
farmer send me away for twenty years, I'll just have to go, that's all.

I always told Naomi I'd do anything in the world for her, and I   24
reckon this will be the time when I've got to prove whether I'm a man of my word or not.

Focusing on the Story

1. Who is the narrator (the character who tells the story), and where is he when he is telling the story? To whom is he talking?
2. Why did the narrator have to be furtive (sneaky) about meeting his girlfriend, Naomi, on Thursday nights? How did they manage to meet?

3. Who is Lud Moseley, and how does he feel about the narrator? Why does he feel this way? How does Mr. John Turner, the farmer the narrator works for, feel about the narrator?
4. Summarize the events that led to Lud Moseley's calico horse, Lightfoot, ending up in Mr. John Turner's stable.
5. How did Betsy get home?
6. How did John Turner respond to Lud Moseley's accusations?

Interpreting and Evaluating

1. Do you feel sympathy toward the narrator? Is he really a common thief, or is he being railroaded by Lud Moseley? Explain.
2. The narrator uses ungrammatical phrases such as "it don't look like it will do much good." How do such phrases together with his actions reveal his character traits? Why does he repeat himself so much? How does the language in the story identify the setting (time and place) of the story?
3. Should the narrator tell the sheriff the whole story? Is he carrying his loyalty to Naomi too far? What would you do in that situation?
4. Based on your own knowledge of human nature, what's the likelihood of Naomi eventually coming to the narrator's rescue? What does your response say about your attitude toward people?
5. What is the main point of this story? Are there any lessons, underlying messages, or themes here, and if so, what are they?

Ideas for Writing and Further Discussion

1. What events led to the narrator's predicament? What could he have done to avoid his arrest? Write an essay in which you explore some of the main mistakes the narrator made that led to his miserable condition, and offer suggestions about how he could have avoided making such mistakes and thus saved himself.
   Suggested *thesis*: two or three such errors and suggestions about how he could have avoided them and what he could have done instead.
   Each *body paragraph* should look at one mistake and give one positive suggestion.

2. Analyze the narrator's character. What character flaws led to his misfortune? Write an essay in which you explore two or three of the narrator's character traits or two or three groups of related traits and show how these qualities or traits led to his predicament.
   Suggested *thesis*: two or three such character traits or groups of traits.
   Each *body paragraph* should look at one trait or groups of related traits and give examples from the story to illustrate how this character trait led to his trouble.

3. One of Benjamin Franklin's epigrams states that honesty is the best policy. Do you agree or disagree with this saying? Take a stand and write an essay in which you agree or disagree with this statement. Give examples from your own experience to support your point.
   Suggested *thesis*: two or three examples that support your point.
   Each *body paragraph* should introduce one such example and show how it proves that honesty is the best policy (or how honesty is not always the best policy if the latter is your point).

4. Have you or someone you know ever been in a similar situation to the narrator's? Describe a time when you or someone you know told a seemingly innocent untruth that led to more serious trouble. How old were you? Why did it seem appropriate to be sneaky at the time? How did the situation escalate? What was the outcome? What lesson did you learn?

   It's not necessary to write a formal thesis statement in a narrative essay, but you may wish to start with a general statement that introduces the event and expresses your attitude toward the experience.

The Schoolteacher's Guest

❖

Isabel Allende

About the Author

Isabel Allende, born in 1942, is Chilean but left her homeland after the U.S.-backed military coup in 1973, in which her uncle, President Salvador Allende, was killed. She now lives near San Francisco.

Something to Think About

Is justice served by demanding an eye for an eye, a tooth for a tooth, and, by extension, a life for a life?

Words to Keep in Mind

weary *(9)* tired

palate *(9)* roof of the mouth

unwavering *(9)* steady

indulge *(9)* to give in to a wish; to be lenient with

vocation *(9)* a call to perform a certain function

viscous *(10)* sticky

pus *(10)* yellowish matter produced by an infection

putrefaction *(10)* rotting

tenacious *(11)* persistent, stubborn

bestowed *(11)* given

arbiter *(18)* person selected to settle a dispute

adobe *(18)* sun-dried clay bricks

mesmerized *(18)* spellbound, hypnotized, fascinated

medlar *(21)* small tree with hard brown fruit

decrepit *(21)* worn out

lurch *(21)* sudden rolling

machete *(23)* large knife with a heavy blade used to cut sugarcane, for example

lethargy *(39)* sluggishness, lack of energy

elation *(39)* extreme joy

furtively *(40)* secretly

malign *(40)* evil, harmful

engendered *(40)* generated

exalted *(45)* filled with pride or joy

complicity *(45)* partnership in wrongdoing

zeal *(45)* intense enthusiasm

T he schoolteacher Inés entered The Pearl of the Orient, deserted at   1
this hour, walked to the counter where Riad Halabí was rolling up a
bolt of bright-flowered cloth, and announced to him that she had just
cut off the head of a guest in her boardinghouse. The merchant took
out his white handkerchief and clapped it to his mouth.

"What did you say, Inés?"   2

"Exactly what you heard, Turk."   3

"Is he dead?"   4

"Of course."   5

"And now what are you going to do?"   6

Reprinted with the permission of Scribner, a division of Simon & Schuster, from *The Stories of Eva Luna* by Isabel Allende. Translated from the Spanish by Margaret Sayers Peden. © 1989 by Isabel Allende. English translation © 1991 by Macmillan Publishing Company.

"That's what I came to ask *you,*" she replied, tucking back a stray   7
lock of hair.

"I think I'd better close the store," sighed Riad Halabí.   8

The two had known each other so long that neither could remem-   9
ber the exact number of years, although both recalled every detail of
the day their friendship had begun. At the time, Halabí had been one
of those salesmen who wander the byways offering their wares, a
commercial pilgrim without compass or fixed course, an Arab immigrant with a false Turkish passport, lonely, weary, with a palate split
like a rabbit's and a subsequent longing to sit in the shadows. She had
been a still-young woman with firm hips and proud shoulders, the
town's only schoolteacher, and the mother of a twelve-year-old son
born of a fleeting love affair. The boy was the center of the schoolteacher's life; she cared for him with unwavering devotion but, barely
masking her inclination to indulge him, applied to him the same
norms of discipline she demanded of the other schoolchildren. She
did not want anyone to be able to say she had brought him up badly;
at the same time, she hoped to negate the father's legacy of wayward-
ness and instead form her son to be of clear mind and generous heart.
The very evening on which Riad Halabí had driven into Agua Santa
from one side of town, from the other a group of boys had carried in
the body of schoolteacher Inés's son on an improvised stretcher. He
had walked onto someone's property to pick up a fallen mango, and
the owner, an outsider whom no one really knew, had fired a blast
from his rifle meaning to scare the boy away but drilling a black hole
in the middle of his forehead through which his life rapidly escaped.
At that moment, the salesman had discovered his vocation for leader-
ship and, without knowing how, had found himself at the center of
things, consoling the mother, organizing the funeral as if he were a
member of the family, and calming the people to prevent them from
tearing the perpetrator limb from limb. Meanwhile, the murderer,
realizing that his life would be worth very little if he remained there,
had fled, meaning never to return.

It was Riad Halabí who the following morning was at the head of   10
the crowd that marched from the cemetery to the place where the boy
had fallen. All the inhabitants of Agua Santa had spent that day hauling mangoes, which they threw through the windows until the house

was filled from floor to ceiling. After a few weeks, the sun had fermented the fruit, which burst open, spilling a viscous juice and impregnating the walls with a golden blood, a sweetish pus, that transformed the dwelling into a fossil of prehistoric dimensions, an enormous beast in process of putrefaction, tormented by the infinite diligence of the larvae and mosquitoes of decomposition.

The death of the boy, the role Riad Halabí had played during   11
those days, and the welcome he had received in Agua Santa, had determined the course of his life. He forgot his nomadic ancestry and remained in the village. There he opened a business, The Pearl of the Orient. He married, was widowed, married a second time, and continued his trade, while his reputation for being a just man steadily increased. Inés, in turn, educated several generations of children with the tenacious affection she would have bestowed upon her son, until her energies were spent; then she stepped aside for teachers who arrived from the city with new primers, and retired. After leaving the schoolroom, she felt as if she had aged suddenly, as if time were accelerating; the days passed so quickly that she could not remember where the hours had gone.

"I go around in a daze, Turk. I'm dying and don't even know it,"   12
she commented.

"You're as healthy as you ever were, Inés," replied Riad   13
Halabí. "The problem is that you're bored. You should not be   14
idle." And he suggested she add a few rooms to her house and take in guests: "We don't have a hotel in this town."

"We don't have tourists, either," she added.   15

"A clean bed and warm breakfast are a blessing for travelers."   16

And so they had been, primarily for the truckdrivers for National   17
Petroleum, who stayed the night in her boardinghouse when the fatigue and tedium of the road had filled their head with hallucinations.

The schoolteacher Inés was the most respected matron in all Agua   18
Santa. She had taught the town's children for several decades, which granted her the authority to intervene in all their lives and take them by the ear when she felt it necessary. Girls brought their boyfriends for her approval, husbands and wives came to her with their marital disagreements; she was counselor, arbiter, and judge in all the town's

problems. Her authority, in fact, was mightier than that of the priest, the doctor, or the police. No one stopped her from the exercise of that power. On one occasion she had stalked into the jail, passed the Lieutenant without speaking, snatched the keys from a nail on the wall, and removed from a cell one of her students who had been jailed after a drunken spree. The officer had tried to stand in her way, but she had shoved him aside and marched the boy outside by the back of his collar. Once in the street, she had given him a couple of smacks and assured him that the next time this happened she would lower his pants and give him a spanking he would never forget. The day that Inés came to tell Riad Halabí she had killed one of her clients, he did not doubt for a moment that she was serious, because he knew her too well. He took her arm and walked with her the two blocks that separated The Pearl of the Orient from her house. It was one of the grandest buildings in town, adobe and wood, with a wide veranda where hammocks were hung during the hottest siestas, and ceiling fans in every room. At that hour the house seemed to be empty; only one guest sat in the parlor drinking beer, mesmerized by the television.

"Where is he?" whispered the Arab merchant.   19

"In one of the back rooms," Inés replied, not even lowering her 20
voice.

She led him to the row of rooms she rented—all joined by an 21
arcade with purple morning-glories climbing the columns and pots of
ferns hanging from the beams—bordering a patio planted with medlar
and banana trees. Inés opened the last door and Riad Halabí entered a
room in deep shadow. The shutters were closed, and it was a moment
before he saw on the bed the corpse of an inoffensive-looking old
man, a decrepit stranger swimming in the puddle of his own death, his
trousers stained with excrement, his head hanging by a strip of ashen
flesh, and wearing a terrible expression of distress, as if apologizing
for all the disturbance and blood, and for the uncommon bother of
having allowed himself to be murdered. Riad Halabí sat down on the
room's only chair, his eyes on the floor, trying to control the lurch of
his stomach. Inés remained standing, arms across her chest, calculating that it would take her two days to wash up the stains and at least
two more to rid the room of its odor of feces and fear.

"How did you do it?" Riad Halabí asked finally, wiping the sweat   22
from his forehead.

"With the machete for harvesting coconuts. I came up behind him   23
and lopped off his head with one swing. He never knew what hit him,
poor man."

"Why?"   24

"I had to do it. It was fate. This old man had very bad luck. He   25
never meant to stop in Agua Santa; he was driving through town and a
rock shattered his windshield. He came to pass a few hours here while
the Italian down at the garage found another windshield. He's
changed a lot—we've all grown older, I guess—but I recognized him
instantly. I've been waiting all these years; I knew he would come
sooner or later. He's the man with the mangoes."

"May Allah protect us," murmured Riad Halabí.   26

"Do you think we should call the Lieutenant?"   27

"Not on your life; why do you say that?"   28

"I'm in the right. He killed my boy."   29

"The Lieutenant wouldn't understand that, Inés."   30

"An eye for an eye and a tooth for a tooth, Turk. Isn't that what   31
your religion teaches?"

"But that's not how the law works, Inés."   32

"Well, then, we can fix him up a little and say he committed sui-   33
cide."

"Don't touch him. How many guests do you have in the house?"   34

"Just that truckdriver. He'll be on his way as soon as it's cool; he   35
has to drive to the capital."

"Good. Don't take in any more guests. Lock the door to this room   36
and wait for me. I'll be back tonight."

"What are you going to do?"   37

"I'll take care of this in my own way."   38

Riad Halabí was sixty-five years old, but he had conserved his   39
youthful vigor and the same spirit that had positioned him at the head
of the throng the day he arrived in Agua Santa. He left the schoolteacher's house and walked rapidly to the first of several visits he was
to make that afternoon. Soon after, a persistent murmur began to
spread through the town. The inhabitants of Agua Santa wakened
from the lethargy of years, excited by the unbelievable news that was
being repeated from house to house, an insuppressible buzzing, infor-

mation that strained to be uttered in shouts, gossip that by the very need to be held to a murmur was conferred special status. Before sunset you could sense in the air the restless elation that for several years would be a characteristic of the town, one incomprehensible to strangers passing through, who could find nothing extraordinary in this town that had the appearance of being an insignificant back-water like so many others on the edge of the jungle. Early in the evening, men began arriving at the tavern; women carried their kitchen chairs out to the sidewalk and sat down to enjoy the cool air; young people gathered en masse in the plaza, as if it were Sunday. The Lieutenant and his men casually made their rounds and then accepted the invitation of the girls at the whorehouse who were celebrating a birthday, they said. By nightfall there were more people in the street than on All Saints' Day; all of them were so studiously occupied in their activities that they seemed to be practicing a part in a movie: some were playing dominoes, others were drinking and smoking on the street corners, some couples were out for a stroll, hand in hand, mothers were running after their children, grandmothers peering nosily from open doorways. The priest lighted the lamps in the parish church and rang the bells signaling a novena to Saint Isidro Martyr, but no one was in the mood for that kind of devotion.

At nine-thirty there was a meeting in the house of schoolteacher Inés: the Turk, the town doctor, and four young men she had taught from the first grade and who were now hefty veterans back from military service. Riad Halabí led them to the back room, where they found the cadaver covered with insects: the window had been left open and it was the hour of the mosquitoes. They stuffed the victim in a canvas sack, wrestled it out to the street, and unceremoniously threw it into the back of Riad Halabí's truck. They drove through the town, right down the main street, waving, as usual, to anyone they happened to see. Some neighbors returned their salutation with more than ordinary enthusiasm, while others pretended not to notice them, furtively giggling, like children surprised at some mischief. Beneath brilliant moonlight the men drove to the spot where many years before the son of the schoolteacher Inés had stooped down for the last time to pick up a mango. The overgrown property sat amid the malign weeds of neglect, decayed by time and bad memories, a tangled hill where mangoes had grown wild, where fruit had dropped from the trees and taken root in the ground, giving birth to new clumps that had in turn engendered others, until an impenetrable jungle had been created that had swallowed up fences, path, even the ruins of the house, of which only a lingering trace of the odor of marmalade remained. The men lighted their kerosene lanterns and plunged into the dense growth, hacking a path with their machetes. When they felt they had gone far enough, one of them pointed to a spot and there, at the foot of a gigantic tree weighed down with fruit, they dug a deep hole in which they deposited the canvas sack. Before shoveling back the dirt, Riad Halabí spoke a brief Muslim prayer, because he knew no other. When they got back to town at midnight, they found that no one had gone to bed; lights were blazing in every window, and people were circulating through the streets.

Meanwhile, the schoolteacher Inés had scrubbed the walls and 41 furniture in the back room with soap and water; she had burned the bedclothing, aired the house, and was waiting for her friends with a fine dinner and a pitcher of rum and pineapple juice. The meal was eaten to the accompaniment of merry chatter about the latest cock-fights—a barbaric sport according to the schoolteacher, but less barbaric, the men alleged, than the bullfights in which a Colombian matador had just lost his liver. Riad Halabí was the last to say good-bye. That night, for the first time in his life, he felt old. At the door, the schoolteacher Inés took his hands and for a moment held them in hers.

"Thank you, Turk," she said. 42

"Why did you come to see me, Inés?" 43

"Because you are the person I love most in this world, and 44 because you should have been the father of my son."

The next day the inhabitants of Agua Santa returned to their usual 45 chores exalted by a magnificent complicity, by a secret kept by good neighbors, one they would guard with absolute zeal and pass down for many years as a legend of justice, until the death of the school-teacher Inés freed us, and now I can tell the story.

 Focusing on the Story

1. How and by whom had the only son of schoolteacher Inés been killed? What did the killer do after the murder? What happened to his house?

2. Who was Riad Halabí, and how did he become involved in the affairs surrounding the death of schoolteacher Inés's son the very day he arrived in Agua Santa? Why did Riad Halabí decide to remain in the village?
3. What did schoolteacher Inés do after she retired from teaching?
4. Describe the people who lived in the town of Agua Santa. How did they feel about schoolteacher Inés? How had she helped them over the years?
5. Who was the old traveler that schoolteacher Inés killed? Who did Inés go to for help? Why weren't the police called?

Interpreting and Evaluating

1. Why do you think the old traveler stopped in Agua Santa? Didn't he recognize the town? Was it fate? Support your opinion.
2. How did many of the townspeople learn about the murder? How did they feel about it? How did they keep it secret? If you had lived in that town, would you have remained silent? Why or why not?
3. Several people helped Inés get rid of the body. What did they do with it? Why did they participate so willingly? Were they common criminals? Explain.
4. What would have happened if Inés or one of the townspeople had called the police? Was there ever a fear that might happen? Why or why not?
5. According to the narrator, the story has been passed down "for many years as a legend of justice." Was justice served in this case? Is justice served by taking the law into your own hands? Would it have been more just to convict and imprison Inés for the murder? Explain.

Ideas for Writing and Further Discussion

1. Do you believe in a predetermined destiny or fate? Write about some aspects of your life that you believe have been shaped by fate. Suggested *thesis*: two or three aspects of your life that you believe have been shaped by fate.
   Each *body paragraph* should explore one such aspect.
2. Our system of justice may not be perfect, but it's better than many judicial systems around the world. Write an essay in which you

discuss two or three aspects of our judicial system that are designed
to make sure that justice is served.
Suggested *thesis*: two or three such aspects.
Each *body paragraph* should take a look at one aspect and show
how it's designed to make sure that justice is served.
3. Or you may take the opposite stand: Our forefathers may have had
the best intentions when they created our judicial system, but it's
slowly falling apart, and today other industrialized countries have a
more efficient system than we do. Write an essay in which you discuss two or three flaws in our judicial system that prevent justice
from being served.
Suggested *thesis*: two or three such flaws.
Each *body paragraph* should look at one such flaw and give several
reasons why it prevents justice from being served.

The Secret

❖

Alberto Moravia

About the Author

Alberto Moravia was born in Rome, Italy, in 1907 and died in 1990. His many novels and short stories often explore human psychology. Novels that have been translated into English include *The Conformist, Contempt*, and *Boredom*.

Something to Think About

Do most people generally get involved in other people's problems today? If you saw someone lying on the sidewalk, would you stop and ask if you could help? Why are most of us afraid to get involved? When are we most likely to get involved?

Words to Keep in Mind

quarry *(2)* place where building stones are cut

daisy *(2)* common flower with many white narrow petals around a yellow center

mull over *(5)* think about; ponder

berth *(5)* place to sleep on a ship or vehicle

gauging *(6)* measuring; estimating

goring *(7)* piercing, especially with a horn or sword

foundling *(10)* child of unknown parents who has been found abandoned

Tiber *(12)* river in Italy that flows through Rome

wrought up *(22)* worked up

D̲on't talk to me about secrets! I had one—and it was the kind that   1
weighs on your conscience like a nightmare.

I am a truck driver. One beautiful spring morning, while hauling a   2
load of lava rock from a quarry near Campagnano to Rome, I ran
square into a man who was coming in the opposite direction on a
motor bike. It was right at the 25 Kilometer marker on the old Cassia
road. Through no fault of his, either. I had kept going on the wrong
side of the road long after having passed a car, and I was speeding; he
was on the right, where he belonged, and going slow. The truck hit
him so hard that I barely had time to see something black fly through
the blue air and then fall and lie still and black against the soft whiteness of a daisy field. The motor bike lay on the other side of the road,
its wheels in the air, like a dead bug.

Lowering my head, I stepped down hard on the gas. I tore down   3
the road to Rome and dropped my load at the yard.

The next day the papers carried the news: So-and-so, forty-three   4
years old, a jobber by trade, leaving a wife and several children, had
been run down at Kilometer 25 of the Cassia road and instantly killed.
Nobody knew who had struck him. The hit-and-run driver had fled
the scene of the accident like a coward. That's exactly what the paper
said: *like a coward.* Except for those three little words that burned a
hole in my brain, it didn't take more than four lines to report on what
was, after all, only the death of a man.

During the next couple of days, I could think of nothing else. I   5
know that I am only a truck driver, but who can claim that truck dri-
vers have no conscience? A truck driver has a lot of time to mull over
his own private business, during the long hours behind the wheel or
lying in the truck's sleeping berth. And when, as in my case, that pri-

From *Roman Tales* by Alberto Moravia. Translated from the Italian by Helen
Cantarella. Reprinted by permission of Curtis Brown Ltd. © 1957 by Casa Editrice
Valentino, Bompiani & Co.

vate business is not all it ought to be, thinking can get to be really pretty tough.

One thing in particular kept nagging at me. I just couldn't under-   6 stand why I hadn't stopped, why I hadn't tried to help the poor guy. I lived the scene over and over again. I would be gauging the distances again before passing that car; I would feel my foot pressing down hard on the accelerator. Then the man's body would come flying up in front of my windshield . . . and at this point I would deliberately block out the picture, as you do at the movies, and I would think, "Now, jam on brakes, jump down, run into the field, pick him up, put him in the bed of the truck and rush him to Santo Spirito Hospital. . . ."

But, you poor fool, you're just dreaming again. I had *not* stopped,   7 I had driven straight on, with head lowered like a bull after a goring.

To make a long story short, the more I thought about that split   8 second when I had stepped on the gas instead of jamming on the brakes, the less I could make it out. Cowardice—that was the word for it all right. But why does a man who has, or at least thinks he has guts, turn into a coward without a moment's warning? That stumped me. Yet the cold hard facts were there: the dead man was really dead; that split second when I might have stopped had passed and was now sinking farther and farther away and no one would ever be able to bring it back. I was no longer the Gino who had passed that car but another Gino who had killed a man and then had run away.

I lay awake nights over it. I grew gloomy and silent and after a   9 while everybody shied away from me at the yard and after work: nobody wants to pass the time with a kill-joy. So I carried my secret around as if it were a hot diamond that you can't entrust to anyone or plant anywhere.

Then, after a while, I began thinking about it less and less and I   10 can even say that there came a time when I didn't think about it at all. But the secret was still stowed away deep down inside me and it weighed on my conscience and kept me from enjoying life. I often thought that I would have felt better if I could have told somebody about it. I wasn't exactly looking for approval—I realized there was no pardon for what I had done—but if I could have told this secret of mine I would have thrown off part of its dead weight onto somebody else who would have helped me carry it. But who could I tell it to? To my friends at the yard? They had other things to worry about. To my family? I had none, being a foundling. My girl friend? She would have been the logical person because, as everybody knows, women are good at understanding you and giving you sympathy when you need it, but unfortunately, I had no girl friend.

II

One Sunday in May I went walking outside the Rome city gates   11
with a girl I had met some time before when I had given her and one of her friends a lift in my truck. She had told me her name and address, and I had seen her again a couple of times. We had enjoyed each other's company, and she had made it clear that she liked me and would be willing to go out with me.

Her name was Iris. She was a lady's maid in the house of some   12
wealthy woman who had lots of servants. I had fallen from the start for her serious little oval face and those great big sad gray eyes of hers. In short, here was just the girl for me in the present circumstances. After we had a cup of coffee at the Exposition Grounds, with all those columns around us, she finally agreed in her shy, silent, and gentle way to go and sit with me in a meadow not far from St. Paul's Gate, where you get a good view of the Tiber and of the new apartment houses lined up on the opposite bank. She had spread out a handkerchief on the grass to keep her skirt from getting dirty and she sat quietly, her legs tucked under her, her hands in her lap, gazing across at the big white buildings on the other side of the river.

I noticed that there were lots of daisies in the grass around us; and   13
like a flash I remembered the soft whiteness of those other daisies among which, just a month earlier, I had seen lying still and dead the man I had struck down. I don't know what got into me but suddenly I couldn't hold back the urge to tell her my secret. If I tell her, I thought, I'll get rid of the load on my chest. She wasn't one of those dizzy, empty-headed girls who, after you've told them a secret, make you feel so much worse than you did before, that you could kick yourself hard for having spilled all you know. She was a nice, understanding person who had doubtless had her share of knocks in life—and they must have been pretty rough knocks if the sad little look on her face meant anything. Just to break the ice, I said to her, in an offhand way: "What are you thinking about, Iris?"

She was just raising her hand to choke back a yawn. Perhaps she 14
was tired. She said: "Nothing."

I didn't let that answer get me down but quickly went on. "Iris, 15
you know that I like you a lot, don't you? That's why I feel that I
shouldn't hide anything from you. You've got to know everything
about me. Iris, I've got a secret."

She kept on looking at the tall buildings on the other side of the 16
river, all the while fingering a little red lump on her chin, a tiny spring
pimple.

"What secret?" she asked. 17

With an effort I got it out: "I've killed a man." 18

She didn't move but kept on poking gently at her chin. Then she 19
shivered all over, as though she had finally understood. "You've
killed a man? And you tell me about it just like that?"

"And how else do you expect me to tell you?" 20

She said nothing. She seemed to be looking for something on the 21
ground. I went on. "Let's get this thing straight. I didn't mean to kill
him."

Suddenly she found what she wanted: picking a long blade of 22
grass, she put it into her mouth and began chewing on it, thoughtfully.
Then, hurriedly, but without hiding anything, I told her about the
accident, bringing out the part about my cowardice. I got pretty
wrought up in spite of myself, but already I was beginning to feel
relieved. I concluded:

"Now tell me what you think about all this." 23

She kept munching on her blade of grass and didn't say a word. 24

I insisted. "I'll bet that now you can't stand the sight of me." 25

I saw her shrug her shoulders, lightly. "And why shouldn't I be 26
able to stand the sight of you?"

"Well, I don't know. After all, it was my fault that poor guy got 27
killed."

"And it bothers you?" 28

"Yes. Terribly." Suddenly, my throat closed tight as if over a hard 29
knot of tears. "I feel as if I can't go on living. No man can go on if he
thinks he's a coward."

"Was it in the papers?" 30

"Yes. They gave it four lines. Just to say he had been killed and 31
that nobody knew who had hit him."

Suddenly she asked, "What time is it?"   32

"Five-fifteen."   33

Another silence. "Listen, Iris, what does a man have to do to find   34
out what's going on in that mind of yours?"

She shifted the blade of grass from one corner of her mouth to the   35
other and said frankly, "Well, if you must know, there's nothing on
my mind. I feel good and I'm not thinking about anything."

I couldn't believe my ears. I protested. "It can't be! You must   36
have been thinking something about something. I'm sure of it."

I saw her smile, faintly. "Well, as a matter of fact, I was thinking   37
about something. But if I tell you, you'll never believe it."

Hopefully, I asked, "Was it about me?"   38

"Good heavens, no! It had absolutely nothing to do with you!"   39

"What was it, then?"   40

She said slowly, "It was just one of those things that only women   41
think about. I was looking at my shoes and seeing that they have holes
in them. I was thinking that there is a big clearance sale on in Via
Cola di Rienzo and that I've got to go there tomorrow and buy myself
a pair of new shoes. There . . . are you satisfied?"

This time I shut up like a clam, my face dark and brooding. She   42
noticed it and exclaimed: "Oh, dear! You're not mad, are you?"

I couldn't help blurting out: "Sure, I'm mad. Damn mad. Here I   43
tell you the secret of my life, and it makes so little impression on you
I wonder why I didn't keep it to myself!"

This bothered her a bit. "No," she said, "I'm glad you told me   44
about it. It really did make an impression on me."

"Well, what kind of an impression?"   45

She thought it over and then said, scrupulously, "Well, I'm sorry   46
that such a thing had to happen to you. It must have been awful!"

"Is that all you've got to say?"   47

"I also think," she added, fingering the pimple on her chin, "that   48
it's only right it should bother you."

"Why?"   49

"Well, you said so yourself. You ought to have stopped to help   50
him but you didn't."

"Then you think I am a coward?"   51

"A coward? Well, yes . . . and then no. After all, a thing like that   52
could happen to anybody."

"But you just said that I ought to have stopped!"   53

"You should have; but you didn't. . . ."   54

At this point I saw her glance down at something in the daisies.   55
"Oh, look! How pretty!"

It was an insect, a green and gold beetle, resting on the white   56
petals of a daisy. Suddenly I felt as if I were emptied out—almost as if
that secret over which I had agonized so long had vanished in the
spring air, carried away, lightly, like the white butterflies that were
flitting around in pairs in the sunlight.

Yet with one dogged last hope, I asked: "But tell me, Iris, in your   57
opinion, was I right or wrong not to stop?"

"You were right and you were wrong. Of course, you ought to   58
have stopped. After all, you had run into him. But, on the other hand,
what good would it have done if you had? He was dead by that time
anyway and you would probably have got into a terrible mess. You
were both right and wrong."

After these words, a thought flashed through my mind. "This is   59
the end of Iris. I'll never take her out again. I thought she was a
bright, understanding girl. Instead, she is really nothing but a half-
wit. Enough is enough." I jumped to my feet.

"Come on, let's go," I said. "Otherwise, we'll be late for the   60
movies."

Once inside the theater, in the dark, she slipped her hand into   61
mine, forcing her fingers through mine. I didn't budge. The film was
a love story, a real tear-jerker. When the lights went on at the end I
saw that her big gray eyes were filled with tears and that her cheeks
were wet. "I just can't help it," she said, patting her face dry with a
handkerchief. "Pictures like this always make me want to cry."

Afterwards we went into a bar and ordered coffee. She pressed so   62
close to me that our bodies touched. Just as the *espresso* machine let
off a loud stream of steam, she said softly, "You know that I really like
you, don't you?" staring at me with those great big beautiful eyes of
hers.

I felt like answering: "Fine. You really like me, but you'll let me   63
carry the whole weight of my secret alone!" Instead, I said nothing.

Now I understood that from her, as from everybody else, I could   64
ask only for affection, nothing more than that.

I answered with a sigh, "I like you a lot, too."   65

But already she had stopped listening to me. She was peering at   66
herself in the mirror behind the bar, absorbed and concerned as she
fingered the little red lump on her chin.

Focusing on the Story

1. After Gino, the truck driver, hit the biker, the motorcycle flew
   through the air and landed in a daisy field. What did the motorbike
   resemble?
2. Why didn't Gino stop to help the biker? Did he deny that it was his
   fault?
3. What bothers Gino about the newspaper article?
4. How does Gino finally try to "get rid of the load on his chest"? Why
   is it so important for him to tell his secret to somebody?
5. How does Iris react when Gino tells her about the accident? Why do
   you think she reacts that way?

Interpreting and Evaluating

1. Is Iris's reaction to Gino's secret similar to or different from Gino's
   reaction after he hit the biker? Explain.
2. When Gino asks Iris if she thinks he is a coward, she is undecided
   and says that "after all, a thing like that could happen to anybody."
   Do you agree that something like this could happen to anybody?
   Explain. What would you do in a similar situation?
3. Although Iris shows little reaction when Gino tells her his secret,
   she cries at the movie. How do you account for that?
4. When people suffer in other parts of the world, we often seem eager
   to help. However, when people are killed in our own cities, most of
   us just sigh, shrug our shoulders, and lock our doors. Why are we
   less likely to get involved in problems that are close to us?
5. Should we care more about the people around us? What happens to
   a society in which no one cares about anyone else?

Ideas for Writing and Further Discussion

1. Write about a time when you should have gotten involved but didn't. Describe what happened and explain why you decided not to get involved. How do you feel about your decision?
2. Write about a time when you did get involved even though people around you chose to do nothing. What happened? Why did you decide to get involved? What was the outcome? Are you glad that you got involved?

   It's not necessary to write a formal thesis statement in a narrative essay, but you may wish to start with a general statement that introduces the event and expresses your attitude toward the experience.

Dealing
with
Adversity

✛

A Letter to God

❖

Gregorio López y Fuentes

About the Author

Gregorio López y Fuentes was a Mexican journalist and author who died in 1966. A son of a farmer and rancher, he was one of Mexico's most acclaimed novelists during the 1930s and received Mexico's National Prize for Literature for his novel *El Indio* in 1935.

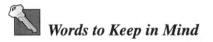 *Something to Think About*

What are some personal attributes or qualities that help people cope with adversity?

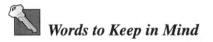 *Words to Keep in Mind*

crest *(1)* high point

corral *(1)* enclosure for keeping animals

centavo *(10)* unit of currency in Mexico and other Latin countries (100 centavos = 1 peso)

hailstones *(11)* frozen raindrops

mortified *(12)* made to feel shame or humiliation

plague *(14)* epidemic disease; disaster

locust *(14)* large grasshopper

resow *(25)* plant again

amiable *(27)* friendly

disillusion *(29)* to take away an illusion or dream; to disappoint

prodigy *(29)* an extraordinary person who inspires wonder

contentment *(31)* satisfaction

T he house—the only one in the entire valley—sat on the crest of a   1
low hill. From this height one could see the river and, next to the corral, the field of ripe corn dotted with the kidney-bean flowers that
always promised a good harvest.

The only thing the earth needed was a rainfall, or at least a   2
shower. Throughout the morning Lencho—who knew his fields inti-
mately—had done nothing else but scan the sky toward the northeast.

"Now we're really going to get some water, woman."   3

The woman, who was preparing supper, replied: 4

"Yes, God willing."   5

The oldest boys were working in the field, while the smaller ones   6
were playing near the house, until the woman called to them all:

"Come for dinner. . . ."   7

It was during the meal that, just as Lencho had predicted, big   8
drops of rain began to fall. In the northeast huge mountains of clouds
could be seen approaching. The air was fresh and sweet.

The man went out to look for something in the corral for no other   9
reason than to allow himself the pleasure of feeling the rain on his
body, and when he returned he exclaimed:

"Those aren't raindrops falling from the sky, they're new coins.   10
The big drops are ten-centavo pieces and the little ones are fives. . . ."

With a satisfied expression he regarded the field of ripe corn with   11
its kidney-bean flowers, draped in a curtain of rain. But suddenly a
strong wind began to blow and together with the rain very large hailstones began to fall. These truly did resemble new silver coins. The
boys, exposing themselves to the rain, ran out to collect the frozen
pearls.

From *Cuentos campesinos de Mexico* (short stories) by Gregorio López y Fuentes.
Translated by Donald A. Yates. © 1940 by Gregorio López y Fuentes. Reprinted with
permission of Angel López Oropeza.

"It's really getting bad now," exclaimed the man, mortified. "I   12
hope it passes quickly."

It did not pass quickly. For an hour the hail rained on the house,   13
the garden, the hillside, the cornfield, on the whole valley. The field
was white, as if covered with salt. Not a leaf remained on the trees.
The corn was totally destroyed. The flowers were gone from the
kidney-bean plants. Lencho's soul was filled with sadness. When the
storm had passed, he stood in the middle of the field and said to his
sons:

"A plague of locusts would have left more than this. . . . The hail   14
has left nothing: this year we will have no corn or beans. . . ."

That night was a sorrowful one: 15

"All our work, for nothing!"   16

"There's no one who can help us!"   17

"We'll all go hungry this year. . . ."   18

But in the hearts of all who lived in that solitary house in the mid-   19
dle of the valley, there was a single hope: help from God.

"Don't be so upset, even though this seems like a total loss.   20
Remember, no one dies of hunger!"

"That's what they say: no one dies of hunger. . . ."   21

All through the night, Lencho thought only of his one hope: the   22
help of God, whose eyes, as he had been instructed, see everything,
even what is deep in one's conscience.

Lencho was an ox of a man, working like an animal in the fields,   23
but still he knew how to write. The following Sunday, at daybreak,
after having convinced himself that there is a protecting spirit, he
began to write a letter which he himself would carry to town and
place in the mail.

It was nothing less than a letter to God.   24

"God," he wrote, "if you don't help me, my family and I will go   25
hungry this year. I need a hundred pesos in order to resow the field
and to live until the crop comes, because the hailstorm . . ."

He wrote "To God" on the envelope, put the letter inside and, still   26
troubled, went to town. At the post office he placed a stamp on the letter and dropped it into the mailbox.

One of the employees, who was a postman and also helped at the   27
post office, went to his boss laughing heartily and showed him the

letter to God. Never in his career as a postman had he known that address. The postmaster—a fat, amiable fellow—also broke out laughing, but almost immediately he turned serious and, tapping the letter on his desk, commented:

"What faith! I wish I had the faith of the man who wrote this let-   28 ter. To believe the way he believes. To hope with the confidence that he knows how to hope with. Starting up a correspondence with God!"

So, in order not to disillusion that prodigy of faith, revealed by a   29 letter that could not be delivered, the postmaster came up with an idea: answer the letter. But when he opened it, it was evident that to answer it he needed something more than goodwill, ink and paper. But he stuck to his resolution: he asked for money from his employee, he himself gave part of his salary, and several friends of his were obliged to give something "for an act of charity."

It was impossible for him to gather together the hundred pesos, so   30 he was able to send the farmer only a little more than half. He put the bills in an envelope addressed to Lencho and with them a letter containing only a single word as a signature: GOD.

The following Sunday Lencho came a bit earlier than usual to ask   31 if there was a letter for him. It was the postman himself who handed the letter to him, while the postmaster, experiencing the contentment of a man who has performed a good deed, looked on from the doorway of his office.

Lencho showed not the slightest surprise on seeing the bills—   32 such was his confidence—but he became angry when he counted the money. . . . God could not have made a mistake, nor could he have denied Lencho what he had requested!

Immediately, Lencho went up to the window to ask for paper and   33 ink. On the public writing table, he started in to write, with much wrinkling of his brow, caused by the effort he had to make to express his ideas. When he finished, he went to the window to buy a stamp which he licked and then affixed to the envelope with a blow of his fist.

The moment that the letter fell into the mailbox the post-master   34 went to open it. It said:

"God: of the money that I asked for, only seventy pesos reached   35 me. Send me the rest, since I need it very much. But don't send it to me through the mail, because the post-office employees are a bunch of crooks. Lencho."

Focusing on the Story

1. Who is Lencho, and why is he waiting for rain?
2. How does Lencho feel when it starts to rain? Why does he see the "raindrops falling from the sky" as "new coins"?
3. How does Lencho feel when the rain turns to hail? What happens to the crops? Who does Lencho turn to for help?
4. When the postman and the postmaster first see Lencho's letter, they break out laughing. Then the postmaster turns serious. Why? What does the postmaster decide to do?
5. How does the postmaster feel about his good deed?
6. Why is Lencho disappointed when he gets the answer? What does he do about it?

Interpreting and Evaluating

1. How do you think the postmaster feels when he reads Lencho's second letter? How would you have felt if you had been the postmaster?
2. The reader learns that "Lencho was an ox of a man working like an animal in the fields, but still he knew how to write." What does this quote say about Lencho? Point out other details from which you can make inferences about Lencho's character as well as his economic and social status.
3. Irony results when the outcome is opposite of what is expected. Explain how the ending is ironic.
4. Should Lencho have been happy with the seventy pesos? Is he greedy and ungrateful, assuming God will do as he commands, or is he a victim of ignorance who takes God's existence too literally?
5. Many readers find the ending humorous. What accounts for the humor? How did you react to the ending?

Ideas for Writing and Further Discussion

1. Lencho's strength, hard work, and confidence will undoubtedly help him succeed according to his expectations. What qualities do you think are important for success? Write an essay in which you discuss two or three qualities that are necessary for success.

Suggested *thesis*: the two or three qualities necessary for success. Each *body paragraph* should explore one of the qualities and show how and why it is important for success.

2. Imagine that you have a rich uncle and that you are his favorite niece or nephew. Write him a letter and ask for money to buy something that you have wanted for a long time. Explain to your uncle what you want, and give several good reasons for why you want it.

A Man Who Had No Eyes

❖

MacKinlay Kantor

About the Author

MacKinlay Kantor was born in Iowa in 1904 and started working for a small Iowa newspaper at age 17. After Hollywood bought his first best-seller, *Long Remember*, he moved to California to work as a screen-writer. His Civil War novel, *Andersonville,* was awarded the Pulitzer Prize. Kantor died in Florida in 1977.

Something to Think About

Some people succeed despite seemingly enormous handicaps. How do they do it?

Words to Keep in Mind

furtive *(2)* secretive, sneaky

splayed *(2)* spread out

malacca stick *(9)* fancy cane or walking stick from Malacca in Malaysia

wheedle *(10)* sweet-talk, persuade

boorish *(11)* rude

inquisitive *(11)* nosy, curious

vat *(18)* big container like a tub

A beggar was coming down the avenue just as Mr. Parsons 1
emerged from his hotel.

He was a blind beggar, carrying the traditional battered cane and 2
thumping his way before him with the cautious, half-furtive effort of
the sightless. He was a shaggy, thick-necked fellow; his coat was
greasy about the lapels and pockets, hand his hand splayed over the
cane's crook with a futile sort of clinging, He wore a black pouch
slung over his shoulder. Apparently he had something to sell.

The air was rich with spring; the sun was warm and yellowed on 3
the asphalt. Mr. Parsons, standing there in front of his hotel and not-
ing the clack-clack approach of the sightless man, felt a sudden and
foolish sort of pity for all blind creatures.

Also, thought Mr. Parsons, he was very glad to be alive. A few 4
years ago he had been little more than a skilled laborer; now he was
successful, respected, admired. . . . Insurance. . . . And he had done it
alone, unaided, struggling beneath handicaps. . . . And he was still
young. The blue air of spring, fresh from its memories of windy pools
and lush shrubbery, could thrill him with eagerness.

He took a step forward just as the tap-tapping blind man passed 5
him by. Quickly the shabby fellow turned.

"Listen, guv'nor. Just a minute of your time." 6

Mr. Parsons said, "It's late. I have an appointment. Do you want 7
me to give you something?"

"I ain't no beggar, guv'nor. You bet I ain't. I got a handy little 8
article here"—he fumbled until he could press a small object into Mr.
Parsons's hand—"that I sell. One buck. Best cigarette lighter made."

Mr. Parsons stood there, somewhat annoyed and embarrassed. He 9
was handsome with his immaculate gray suit and gray hat and
malacca stick. Of course the man with the cigarette lighters could not
see him. . . . "But I don't smoke," he said.

"A Man Who Had No Eyes" by MacKinlay Kantor, copyright 1931 by *Liberty*.

"Listen. I bet you know plenty people who smoke. Nice little pres- 10
ent," wheedled the man. "And mister, you wouldn't mind helping a
poor guy out?" He clung to Mr. Parsons's sleeve as he waited for the
answer.

Mr. Parsons sighed and felt in his vest pocket. He brought out two 11
half dollars and pressed them into the man's hand. "Certainly, I'll
help you out. As you say, I can give it to someone. Maybe the elevator
boy would—" He hesitated, not wishing to be boorish and inquisitive,
even with a blind peddler. "Have you lost your sight entirely?"

The shabby man pocketed the two half dollars. "Fourteen years, 12
guv'nor." Then he added, with an insane sort of pride, "Westbury, sir.
I was one of 'em."

"Westbury," repeated Mr. Parsons. "Ah, yes. The chemical explo- 13
sion. . . . The papers haven't mentioned it for years. But at the time it
was supposed to be one to the greatest disasters in—"

"They've all forgot about it." The fellow shifted his weight 14
wearily. "I tell you, guv'nor, a man who was in it don't forget about it.
Last thing I ever saw was C shop going up in one grand smudge and
that awful gas pouring in at all the busted windows."

Mr. Parsons coughed, but the blind peddler was caught up with 15
the train of his one dramatic reminiscence. Also, he was thinking that
there might be more half dollars in Mr. Parsons's pocket.

"Just think about it guv'nor. There was a hundred and eight peo- 16
ple killed, about two hundred injured, and over fifty of them lost their
eyes. Blind as bats—" He groped forward until his dirty hand rested
against Mr. Parsons's coat. "I tell you, sir, there wasn't nothing worse
than that in the war. If I had lost my eyes in that war, okay. I would
have been well took care of. But I was just a workman, working for
what was in it. And I got it. You're so right I got it, while the capital-
ists were making their dough! They was insured, don't worry about
that. They—"

"Insured," repeated his listener. "Yes. That's what I sell—"   17

"You want to know how I lost my eyes?" cried the man. "Well, 18
here it is!" His words fell with the bitter and studied drama of a story
often told, and told for money. "I was there in C shop, last of all the
folks rushing out. Out in the air there was a chance, even with buildings exploding right and left. A lot of guys made it safe out the door

and got away. And just when I was about there, crawling along between those big vats, a guy behind me grabs my leg. He says, 'Let me past, you—!' Maybe he was nuts. I dunno. I try to forgive him in my heart, guv'nor. But he was bigger than me. He hauls me back and climbs right over me! Tramples me into the dirt. And he gets out, and I lie there with all that poison gas pouring down on all sides of me, and flame and stuff. . . ." He swallowed—a studied sob—and stood dumbly expectant. He could imagine the next words: *Tough luck, my man. Awfully tough. Now, I want to*— "That's the story, gov'nor."

The spring wind shrilled past them, damp and quivering.   19

"Not quite," said Mr. Parsons.   20

The blind peddler shivered crazily. "Not quite? What do you mean, you—?"   21

"The story is true," Mr. Parsons said, "except that it was the other way around."   22

"Other way around?" He croaked unamiably. "Say, guv'nor—"   23

"I was in C shop," said Mr. Parsons. "It was the other way around. You were the fellow who hauled back on me and climbed over me. You were bigger than I was, Markwardt."   24

The blind man stood for a long time, swallowing hoarsely. He gulped: "Parsons. By heaven! By heaven! I thought you—" And then he screamed fiendishly: "Yes. Maybe so. Maybe so. But I'm blind! I'm blind, and you've been standing there letting me spout to you, and laughing at me every minute! I'm blind!"   25

People in the street turned to stare at him.   26

"You got away, but I'm blind! Do you hear, I'm—"   27

"Well," said Mr. Parsons, "don't make such a row about it, Markwardt. So am I."   28

Focusing on the Story

1. Describe Mr. Parsons's appearance. Does he seem satisfied with his life? Does he seem successful?
2. Describe the blind beggar that Mr. Parsons encounters outside his hotel? How does Mr. Parsons know that the beggar is blind?
3. What does the beggar want from Mr. Parsons? What is the beggar peddling or selling?

4. How does Mr. Parsons feel about the beggar at first? How does his attitude change after he learns who the beggar is?
5. How has the beggar lost his eyesight?
6. The beggar tells Mr. Parsons the sequence of events that led to his blindness. Relate his story. Is his story accurate? What really happened?

Interpreting and Evaluating

1. How does Mr. Parsons recognize the beggar as Mr. Markwardt?
2. How do you feel about Mr. Markwardt?
3. How does Mr. Parsons's attitude toward life and his handicap differ from that of Mr. Markwardt?
4. Why do some people seem to succeed despite serious handicaps while others succumb to them?

Ideas for Writing and Further Discussion

1. Do you know people with physical handicaps? How do they handle their disabilities? Are some of them successful? Write a paragraph or two about someone you know with a physical disability. How do you feel about this person? Start with a sentence that states your attitude toward the person and include details about his or her personality that support your feeling.
2. Imagine that you have a physical disability. You may, for example, imagine that you are in a wheelchair or you may be blind and have to walk with a white cane. What would you do? Write one or several paragraphs in which you discuss two or three ways that would help you cope.
3. Although Mr. Parsons and Mr. Markwardt have similar disabilities as a result of a chemical explosion, they differ in most other ways. Their appearances, for example, are different, and they have different attitudes. Write a short essay in which you discuss several differences between the two men.
   Suggested *thesis*: several ways the two blind men differ.
   Each *body paragraph* should explore one such way.

The Necklace

❖

Guy de Maupassant

About the Author

Born into the French nobility in 1850, Guy de Maupassant grew up to be a brilliant novelist and short story writer. With his quick character sketches, dramatic plots, and surprise endings, he is regarded as one of the most skillful short story writers of all time. He died in a private insane asylum in Paris at age forty-three.

Something to Think About

Do money and material possessions automatically lead to happiness? What makes a person content?

Words to Keep in Mind

dowry *(1)* property that a woman brings to a man at marriage

caste *(2)* social class restricted by birth

suppleness *(2)* adaptability to different ideas and circumstances

Breton *(3)* a native of Brittany; a region in western France

antechambers *(3)* smaller rooms that lead into larger rooms

inestimable *(3)* of too great a value to be measured; invaluable

frock *(5)* dress

chagrin *(6)* feeling of embarrassment

elated *(7)* filled with joy

stupefied *(18)* overwhelmed with amazement

dismay *(18)* fear

vexation *(20)* irritation

ecstasy *(40)* extreme happiness

homage *(45)* respect; honor

mantle *(57)* sleeveless coat, cape; cover

clasp *(70)* a fastening, such as a hook or buckle, holding two parts together

francs, louis, sous *(26, 80, 85)* French monetary units

usurer *(80)* a money lender who charges illegally high interest

mansard roof *(84)* common roof in Europe with two slopes on each side; the lower slope is almost vertical

S he was one of those pretty, charming young ladies, born, as if 1 through an error of destiny, into a family of clerks. She had no dowry, no hopes, no means of becoming known, appreciated, loved and married by a man either rich or distinguished; and she allowed herself to marry a petty clerk in the office of the Board of Education.

She was simple, not being able to adorn herself, but she was 2 unhappy, as one out of her class; for women belong to no caste, no race, their grace, their beauty and their charm serving them in the place of birth and family. Their inborn finesse, their instinctive elegance, their suppleness of wit, are their only aristocracy, making some daughters of the people the equal of great ladies.

She suffered incessantly, feeling herself born for all delicacies 3 and luxuries. She suffered from the poverty of her apartment, the shabby walls, the worn chairs and the faded stuffs. All these things, which another woman of her station would not have noticed, tortured and angered her. The sight of the little Breton servant, who cleaned this humble home, awoke in her sad regrets and desperate dreams.

She thought of quiet antechambers with their oriental hangings lighted by high bronze torches and of the two great footmen in short trousers who sleep in the large armchairs, made sleepy by the heavy air from the heating apparatus. She thought of large drawing rooms hung in old silks, of graceful pieces of furniture carrying bric-a-brac of inestimable value and of the little perfumed coquettish apartments made for five o'clock chats with most intimate friends, men known and sought after, whose attention all women envied and desired.

When she seated herself for dinner before the round table, where 4 the tablecloth had been used three days, opposite her husband who uncovered the tureen with a delighted air, saying: "Oh! the good pot-pie! I know nothing better than that," she would think of the elegant dinners, of the shining silver, of the tapestries peopling the walls with ancient personages and rare birds in the midst of fairy forests; she thought of the exquisite food served on marvelous dishes, of the whispered gallantries, listened to with the smile of the Sphinx while eating the rose-colored flesh of the trout or a chicken's wing.

She had neither frocks nor jewels, nothing. And she loved only 5 those things. She felt that she was made for them. She had such a desire to please, to be sought after, to be clever and courted.

She had a rich friend, a schoolmate at the convent, whom she did 6 not like to visit; she suffered so much when she returned. And she wept for whole days from chagrin, from regret, from despair and disappointment.

One evening her husband returned, elated, bearing in his hand a 7 large envelope.

"Here," he said, "here is something for you."   8

She quickly tore open the wrapper and drew out a printed card on 9 which were inscribed these words:

The Minister of Public Instruction and Madame George 10 *Ramponneau ask the honor of M. and Mme Loisel's company Monday evening, January 18, at the Minister's residence.*

Instead of being delighted, as her husband had hoped, she threw 11 the invitation spitefully upon the table, murmuring:

"What do you suppose I want with that?"   12

"But, my dearie, I thought it would make you happy. You never 13 go out, and this is an occasion, and a fine one! I had a great deal of trouble to get it. Everybody wishes one, and it is very select; not many are given to employees. You will see the whole official world there."

She looked at him with an irritated eye and declared impatiently: 14

"What do you suppose I have to wear to such a thing as that?"   15

He had not thought of that; he stammered: 16

"Why, the dress you wear when we go to the theater. It seems   17
very pretty to me."

He was silent, stupefied, in dismay, at the sight of his wife weep-   18
ing. Two great tears fell slowly from the corners of her eyes toward
the corners of her mouth; he stammered:

"What is the matter? What is the matter?"   19

By a violent effort she had controlled her vexation and responded   20
in a calm voice, wiping her moist cheeks:

"Nothing. Only I have no dress and consequently I cannot go to   21
this affair. Give your invitation to some colleague whose wife is better fitted out than I."

He was grieved but answered: 22

"Let us see, Matilda. How much would a suitable gown cost,   23
something that would serve for other occasions, something very
simple?"

She reflected for some seconds, making estimates and thinking of   24
a sum that she could ask for without bringing with it an immediate
refusal and a frightened exclamation from the economical clerk.

Finally she said in a hesitating voice: 25

"I cannot tell exactly, but it seems to me that four hundred francs   26
ought to cover it."

He turned a little pale, for he had saved just this sum to buy a gun   27
that he might be able to join some hunting parties the next summer,
on the plains at Nanterre, with some friends who went to shoot larks
up there on Sunday. Nevertheless, he answered:

"Very well. I will give you four hundred francs. But try to have a   28
pretty dress."

The day of the ball approached, and Mme Loisel seemed sad, dis-   29
turbed, anxious. Nevertheless, her dress was nearly ready. Her husband said to her one evening:

"What is the matter with you? You have acted strangely for two or   30
three days."

And she responded: "I am vexed not to have a jewel, not one 31
stone, nothing to adorn myself with. I shall have such a poverty-laden
look. I would prefer not to go to this party."

He replied: "You can wear some natural flowers. At this season 32
they look very chic. For ten francs you can have two or three magnificent roses."

She was not convinced. "No," she replied, "there is nothing more 33
humiliating than to have a shabby air in the midst of rich women."

Then her husband cried out: "How stupid we are! Go and find 34
your friend Madame Forestier and ask her to lend you her jewels. You
are well enough acquainted with her to do this."

She uttered a cry of joy. "It is true!" she said. "I had not thought 35
of that."

The next day she took herself to her friend's house and related her 36
story of distress. Mme Forestier went to her closet with the glass
doors, took out a large jewel case, brought it, opened it and said:
"Choose, my dear."

She saw at first some bracelets, then a collar of pearls, then a 37
Venetian cross of gold and jewels and of admirable workmanship.
She tried the jewels before the mirror, hesitated, but could neither
decide to take them nor leave them. Then she asked:

"Have you nothing more?" 38

"Why, yes. Look for yourself. I do not know what will please 39
you."

Suddenly she discovered in a black satin box a superb necklace of 40
diamonds, and her heart beat fast with an immoderate desire. Her
hands trembled as she took them up. She placed them about her
throat, against her dress, and remained in ecstasy before them. Then
she asked in a hesitating voice full of anxiety:

"Could you lend me this? Only this?" 41

"Why, yes, certainly." 42

She fell upon the neck of her friend, embraced her with passion, 43
then went away with her treasure.

The day of the ball arrived. Mme Loisel was a great success. She 44
was the prettiest of all, elegant, gracious, smiling and full of joy. All
the men noticed her, asked her name and wanted to be presented. All
the members of the Cabinet wished to waltz with her. The minister of
education paid her some attention.

She danced with enthusiasm, with passion, intoxicated with plea- 45
sure, thinking of nothing, in the triumph of her beauty, in the glory of
her success, in a kind of cloud of happiness that came of all this
homage and all this admiration, of all these awakened desires and this
victory so complete and sweet to the heart of woman.

She went home toward four o'clock in the morning. Her husband 46
had been half asleep in one of the little salons since midnight with
three other gentlemen whose wives were enjoying themselves very
much.

He threw around her shoulders the wraps they had carried for the 47
coming home, modest garments of everyday wear, whose poverty
clashed with the elegance of the ball costume. She felt this and
wished to hurry away in order not to be noticed by the other women
who were wrapping themselves in rich furs.

Loisel detained her. "Wait," said he. "You will catch cold out 48
there. I am going to call a cab."

But she would not listen and descended the steps rapidly. When 49
they were in the street they found no carriage, and they began to seek
for one, hailing the coachmen whom they saw at a distance.

They walked along toward the Seine, hopeless and shivering. 50
Finally they found on the dock one of those old nocturnal coupés that
one sees in Paris after nightfall, as if they were ashamed of their misery by day.

It took them as far as their door in Martyr Street, and they went 51
wearily up to their apartment. It was all over for her. And on his part
he remembered that he would have to be at the office by ten o'clock.

She removed the wraps from her shoulders before the mirror for a 52
final view of herself in her glory. Suddenly she uttered a cry. Her
necklace was not around her neck.

Her husband, already half undressed, asked: "What is the mat- 53
ter?"

She turned toward him excitedly: 54

"I have—I have—I no longer have Madame Forestier's neck- 55
lace."

He arose in dismay: "What! How is that? It is not possible." 56

And they looked in the folds of the dress, in the folds of the man- 57
tle, in the pockets, everywhere. They could not find it.

He asked: "You are sure you still had it when we left the house?" 58

"Yes, I felt it in the vestibule as we came out."   59

"But if you had lost it in the street we should have heard it fall. It   60
must be in the cab."

"Yes. It is probable. Did you take the number?"   61

"No. And you, did you notice what it was?"   62

"No."   63

They looked at each other, utterly cast down. Finally Loisel   64
dressed himself again.

"I am going," said he, "over the track where we went on foot, to   65
see if I can find it."

And he went. She remained in her evening gown, not having the   66
force to go to bed, stretched upon a chair, without ambition or
thoughts.

Toward seven o'clock her husband returned. He had found noth-   67
ing.

He went to the police and to the cab offices and put an advertise-   68
ment in the newspapers, offering a reward; he did everything that
afforded them a suspicion of hope.

She waited all day in a state of bewilderment before this frightful   69
disaster. Loisel returned at evening, with his face harrowed and pale,
and had discovered nothing.

"It will be necessary," said he, "to write to your friend that you   70
have broken the clasp of the necklace and that you will have it
repaired. That will give us time to turn around."

She wrote as he dictated.   71

At the end of a week they had lost all hope. And Loisel, older by   72
five years, declared:

"We must take measures to replace this jewel."   73

The next day they took the box which had inclosed it to the jew-   74
eler whose name was on the inside. He consulted his books.

"It is not I, madame," said he, "who sold this necklace; I only fur-   75
nished the casket."

Then they went from jeweler to jeweler, seeking a necklace like   76
the other one, consulting their memories, and ill, both of them, with
chagrin and anxiety.

In a shop of the Palais-Royal they found a chaplet of diamonds   77
which seemed to them exactly like the one they had lost. It was valued at forty thousand francs. They could get it for thirty-six thousand.

They begged the jeweler not to sell it for three days. And they   78
made an arrangement by which they might return it for thirty-four
thousand francs if they found the other one before the end of
February.

Loisel possessed eighteen thousand francs which his father had   79
left him. He borrowed the rest.

He borrowed it, asking for a thousand francs of one, five hundred   80
of another, five louis of this one and three louis of that one. He gave
notes, made ruinous promises, took money of usurers and the whole
race of lenders. He compromised his whole existence, in fact, risked
his signature without even knowing whether he could make it good or
not, and, harassed by anxiety for the future, by the black misery
which surrounded him and by the prospect of all physical privations
and moral torture, he went to get the new necklace, depositing on the
merchant's counter thirty-six thousand francs.

When Mme Loisel took back the jewels to Mme Forestier the lat-   81
ter said to her in a frigid tone:

"You should have returned them to me sooner, for I might have   82
needed them."

She did not open the jewel box as her friend feared she would. If   83
she should perceive the substitution what would she think? What
should she say? Would she take her for a robber?

Mme Loisel now knew the horrible life of necessity. She did her   84
part, however, completely, heroically. It was necessary to pay this
frightful debt. She would pay it. They sent away the maid; they
changed their lodgings; they rented some rooms under a mansard
roof.

She learned the heavy cares of a household, the odious work of a   85
kitchen. She washed the dishes, using her rosy nails upon the greasy
pots and the bottoms of the stewpans. She washed the soiled linen, the
chemises and dishcloths, which she hung on the line to dry; she took
down the refuse to the street each morning and brought up the water,
stopping at each landing to breathe. And, clothed like a woman of the
people, she went to the grocer's, the butcher's and the fruiterer's with
her basket on her arm, shopping, haggling to the last sou her miserable money.

Every month it was necessary to renew some notes, thus obtain-   86
ing time, and to pay others.

The husband worked evenings, putting the books of some mer- 87
chants in order, and nights he often did copying at five sous a page.

And this life lasted for ten years. 88

At the end of ten years they had restored all, all, with interest of 89
the usurer, and accumulated interest, besides.

Mme Loisel seemed old now. She had become a strong, hard 90
woman, the crude woman of the poor household. Her hair badly
dressed, her skirts awry, her hands red, she spoke in a loud tone and
washed the floors in large pails of water. But sometimes, when her
husband was at the office, she would seat herself before the window
and think of that evening party of former times, of that ball where she
was so beautiful and so flattered.

How would it have been if she had not lost that necklace? Who 91
knows? Who knows? How singular is life and how full of changes!
How small a thing will ruin or save one!

One Sunday, as she was taking a walk in the Champs Elysées to rid 92
herself of the cares of the week, she suddenly perceived a woman
walking with a child. It was Mme Forestier, still young, still pretty,
still attractive. Mme Loisel was affected. Should she speak to her? Yes,
certainly. And now that she had paid, she would tell her all. Why not?

She approached her. "Good morning, Jeanne." 93

Her friend did not recognize her and was astonished to be so 94
familiarly addressed by this common personage. She stammered:

"But, madame—I do not know—You must be mistaken." 95

"No, I am Matilda Loisel." 96

Her friend uttered a cry of astonishment: "Oh! my poor Matilda! 97
How you have changed."

"Yes, I have had some hard days since I saw you, and some miser- 98
able ones—and all because of you."

"Because of me? How is that?" 99

"You recall the diamond necklace that you loaned me to wear to 100
the minister's ball?"

"Yes, very well." 101

"Well, I lost it." 102

"How is that, since you returned it to me?" 103

"I returned another to you exactly like it. And it has taken us ten 104
years to pay for it. You can understand that it was not easy for us who
have nothing. But it is finished, and I am decently content."

Mme Forestier stopped short. She said: 105
"You say that you bought a diamond necklace to replace mine?"   106
"Yes. You did not perceive it then? They were just alike."   107
And she smiled with a proud and simple joy. Mme Forestier was   108
touched and took both her hands as she replied:
"Oh, my poor Matilda! Mine were false. They were not worth   109
over five hundred francs!"

Focusing on the Story

1. What is the setting (time and place) of the story? How would you
   describe the Loisels' lifestyle before the loss of the necklace? How
   does it change after the loss?
2. What kind of person is Matilda Loisel before she loses her friend's
   necklace? How does she feel about herself? Is she attractive? Why
   isn't she happy? Is she spoiled? How does she change during the ten
   years after the loss of the necklace?
3. How would you characterize the relationship between Mr. and Mrs.
   Loisel before and after the loss of the necklace? How does Mr.
   Loisel treat his wife? How does she respond?

Interpreting and Evaluating

1. After the loss of the necklace, appearance and social status seem
   less important to Matilda. Why?
2. How has the hard work affected Matilda's character? How has her
   attitude changed at the end of the story? How has her relationship
   with her husband changed?
3. What, if anything, has Matilda learned from her experience? Does
   she feel better about herself? Is she more content? Explain.
4. Should Matilda have told her rich friend about the loss of the necklace right away? How might Matilda's life have been different if she
   had? What would you have done in a similar situation?
5. Maupassant writes, "How singular is life and how full of changes!
   How small a thing will ruin or save one!" What does the author
   mean by these statements? Has Matilda been ruined or saved?

6. The ancient Greek physician Hippocrates once said that idleness leads to evil. What does this mean? Do you agree? Explain.
7. Some have accused Guy Maupassant of being a misogynist, or someone who hates women. What, if anything, in the story might support this allegation or accusation?

Ideas for Writing and Further Discussion

1. Write an essay in which you discuss how Matilda Loisel's life changes after she loses her friend's necklace. Compare her life before the loss with her life after the loss, and point out how the changes help her focus on the more important things in life. Suggested *thesis*: several ways that Matilda Loisel changes. Each *body paragraph* should explore one way.
2. What makes you happy? Write a paragraph or two about some things that put a smile on your face.
3. Has a seemingly small event ever changed the course of your life? Have you, for example, like the main character in Maupassant's story, lost something important to you? Perhaps you've even had an accident, or perhaps you met someone by chance. Write about a chance event that changed something in your life. Describe what happened, and explain how the event changed your life. Did it change your life for the better or worse?

Myths,
Legends,
and
Tales

❖

The Beggarwoman of Locarno

❖

Heinrich von Kleist
(translated by Martin Greenberg)

About the Author

Heinrich von Kleist, who was born in Frankfurt, Germany, in 1777, wrote short stories and plays that often explore the failure of reason and human beings' penchant for injustice, especially when they are in charge. Kleist died in 1811.

Something to Think About

Cruelty to others often goes unpunished. However, even if society fails to punish malicious behavior, does our conscience make us suffer?

Words to Keep in Mind

marquis *(1)* nobleman ranking below a duke and above an earl or count

groan *(1)* cry out

in straitened circumstances *(2)* needing money badly

audibly *(2)* something that can be clearly heard

chagrin *(4)* embarrassment, disappointment

marquise *(4)* the wife or widow of a marquis

witching hour *(4)* midnight; the time when witches assemble to cele-
brate their rituals and sorcery

At the foot of the Alps, near Locarno in northern Italy, stood an   1
ancient castle belonging to a Marquis, which today, coming down the
St. Gotthard, one sees in ruins. In one of the great, high-ceilinged
rooms, the mistress of the house one day spread a bed of straw out of
pity for a sick old woman who had come begging to her door. When
the Marquis returned from hinting, he happened to walk into this
room, where he kept his shotgun. Irritably he ordered the woman to
get up out of the corner where she was lying and find herself a place
behind the stove. As she rose, the woman slipped with her crutch on
the polished floor and fell, injuring her spine so seriously that it was
only with an immense effort that she was able to get up again and
cross the room as she had been bidden. But once behind the stove she
collapsed, groaning and sighing, and died.

Several years later, when war and bad harvests had brought the   2
Marquis into straitened circumstances, there appeared a Florentine
knight who liked the castle's beautiful location and offered to buy it.
The Marquis, who was extremely eager to sell, told his wife to put the
stranger up in the unoccupied room mentioned above, which was furnished very splendidly. But imagine the couple's dismay when the
knight came downstairs, pale and shaken, in the middle of the night
and swore the room was haunted. Something invisible to the eye, he
said, had got up from the corner with a rusting sound, as if from a bed
of straw, quite audibly crossed the room with slow and feeble steps,
and collapsed, groaning and sighing, behind the stove.

The Marquis, frightened, without knowing why himself, laughed   3
at the knight with forced heartiness, and offered to get up on the post
and pass the night with him in the room, if that would set his mind at
rest. However, the knight asked him to be good enough to let him

---

"The Beggarwoman of Locarno" by Heinrich von Kleist. From *The Marquise of O &
Other Stories* by Heinrich von Kleist, translation by Martin Greenberg (Criterion
Books). Introduction and English translation of the stories copyright 1960 by Martin
Greenberg. Reprinted by permission of HarperCollins.

spend the rest of the night in an armchair in the Marquis' bedroom, and when morning came he called for his coach, paid his respects, and left.

This incident, which created a great sensation, frightened away 4 several prospective buyers, much to the Marquis' chagrin. When, oddly and inexplicably, it began to be whispered even among his own people that a ghost walked the room at midnight, he decided to investigate the matter himself, so as to put an end, once and for all, to the rumors. At nightfall, he had his bed made up in the room and waited, wide awake, for midnight to come. Imagine his dismay when, at the witching hour, he heard the mysterious noise. It was as if someone got up from a heap of rustling straw, crossed the room, and collapsed, sighing and gasping, behind the stove. The next morning, when he came downstairs, the Marquise asked how his investigation had tuned out. When he looked around him apprehensively and, after bolting the door, assured her there actually was a ghost, she was frightened as never before in her life. She begged him not to utter a word about it before he had made another trial of the matter, quite coolly, with her. That night, however, they, as well as the faithful servant who accompanied them, heard the same inexplicable ghostly noise. Only their pressing desire to get rid of the castle at any price enabled them to stifle their terror in the presence of the servant and blame the thing on some petty, accidental cause that would certainly come to light.

On the evening of the third day, when the two, with pounding 5 hearts, again climbed the stairs to the guest room, resolved to get to the bottom of the business, they discovered the watchdog, whom somebody had unchained, in front of the door. Without knowing exactly why, perhaps from an instinctive desire to have the company of some third living creature, they took the dog into the room with them.

Around eleven o'clock, with two candlesticks burning on the 6 table, the couple sat down on separate beds, the Marquise fully clothed, the Marquis with sword and pistols, which he had taken from the closet, at his side. While they tried as best they could to pass the time in conversation, the dog curled up in the center of the floor and went to sleep. Then, at the stoke of midnight, the dreadful noise was heard again. Somebody whom no human eye could see got up on crutches in the corner of the room. There was the sound of straw rusting under him; and at the first step: tap! tap! the dog awakened, started to its feet with its ears pricked up, and backed away to the stove, growling and barking, as if somebody were walking toward it. At this sight, the Marquise, her hair standing on end, plunged from the room. The Marquis seized his sword and shouted, "Who's there?", slashing the air like a maniac in every direction. When there was no answer, the Marquise called for her coach, determined to drive to town that instant. But before she had even clattered to the gate, after snatching up a few belongings, she saw the castle go up in flames all around her. The Marquis, maddened with terror, had caught up a candle and, weary of his life, set fire to every corner of the place, which was paneled in wood throughout. Vainly, she sent people in to save the unfortunate man, but he had already perished in the most pitiful way. Even today his white bones, which the country people gathered together, rest in the corner of the room from which he had ordered the beggarwoman of Locarno to get up.

Focusing on the Story

1. Describe the house where the Marquis and Marquise lived. Where was the house located? What does it look like at the time when the story is told?
2. Who was the woman who died behind the stove in one of the upstairs bedrooms?
3. What was the cause of the woman's death?
4. What happened to the Marquis' fortune in the years following the death of the old woman? Why was it necessary to sell the house?
5. What happened to the first prospective buyer? Why did he decide to leave?
6. What did the Marquis experience when he slept in the room where the old woman had died?
7. How did the Marquis and Marquise spend the three subsequent nights?
8. What happened to the Marquis and Marquise at the end of the story?

Interpreting and Evaluating

1. After spending the night at the castle, the buyer decided to leave. Did he make the right decision?
2. The author of this story, Heinrich von Kleist, is known for his psychological insight. What psychological phenomena could the castle and the ghost of the dead woman represent?
3. "The Beggarwoman of Locarno" also explores other phenomena such as superstition, fright, and desperation. What does the author, who incidentally himself committed suicide at the age of 34, have to say about these common human experiences?

Ideas for Writing and Further Discussion

1. Do you know any ghost stories? In a paragraph or two retell an old ghost story you have heard. Where and when did the story take place? Were real people involved? What happened?
2. Do you believe in the supernatural? Have you or someone you know ever had a supernatural experience? What happened? Write an essay about a supernatural experience you or someone you know once had. When and where did the incident occur? Was anyone else involved? How did you or your friend feel about the occurrence?
3. What are your fears? Are you, for example, afraid of ghosts, the boogieman or simply the dark? Do loud noises or natural phenomena such as thunder and lightning, earthquakes, and fires frighten you? Write an essay in which you discuss several phenomena or happenings that scare you and explain why you think they are so terrifying.
   Suggested *thesis*: three or four incidents that frighten you.
   Each *body paragraph* should explore one such incident and explain why it is so scary.

Frigga's Necklace

❖

Retold by Catharine F. Sellew Hinchman

About the Author

Catharine F. Sellew Hinchman is an American writer. Her books include *Adventures with the Gods* and *Adventures with the Heroes.*

Something to Think About

A seemingly small event can sometimes lead to disaster. How does the goddess Frigga in this story cause storms, cold weather, ice, and snow to enter the world?

Words to Keep in Mind

Odin *(1)* head of all the Norse gods, also called All-father

Frigga *(1)* Odin's wife and mother of the gods

Asgard *(3)* home of the Norse gods

Frigga, the queen of the gods, sat beside Odin on the high throne on the top of the world. She was very beautiful, with white plumes in her hair that waved softly in the breeze. She wore snowy white robes 1

From *Adventures with the Giants* by Catharine F. Sellew Hinchman, © 1950 by Catharine F. Sellew Hinchman. Reprinted by permission of Little, Brown and Company, Boston.

and a golden girdle from which hung a ring of keys. She smiled down at the men and women of the earth and watched over their homes and children.

Often she feasted with the other gods and goddesses, but best of all she loved to spin golden thread and weave clouds of glowing colors to put in the sky. Her spinning wheel was set with jewels that sparkled at night. The people of the earth saw them shining in the sky and called them stars. 2

Frigga was kind and beautiful, but she was also very vain. She loved new gowns and bright jewelry. She could not be happy unless she was the most beautifully dressed goddess in Asgard. 3

One day she took out her box of jewels and looked at one necklace after another. None of them were quite brilliant enough or quite the right length. None of them really suited her new gown. She wanted a new necklace. 4

It should be a necklace of pure gold, she decided. It should be made in such a design that everyone—especially her husband, Odin—would wonder at it. So Frigga sent a messenger down to the workshop of the dwarfs. Those ugly little blacksmiths could make magic things out of the metals and jewels that they dug from the heart of the mountains. 5

Frigga's messenger went to the most skillful of the dwarfs, and told him what the queen of the gods wanted. 6

"It must be more beautiful than anything you have ever made," the messenger commanded. 7

"And all of gold?" asked the dwarf. 8

"Yes, pure gold. You must not use any other metal." 9

"But we do not have enough gold for such a necklace," said the dwarf, shaking his head sadly. 10

"Then dig deeper into the heart of the mountains until you have found enough. This is an order from Frigga! It is the goddess queen who demands it!" 11

"I know! I know! But we have already made many ornaments of gold for that beautiful lady and the other gods and goddesses. We have only a little gold left. Please explain this to her highness. Tell her I will make a necklace of wondrous beauty. It will be made of all the metals of the earth in a design worthy only of the lovely Frigga!" 12

When the messenger went back and told Frigga what the most   13
skillful dwarf had said she was very disappointed. A necklace of
many metals would no doubt be beautiful. But for her new gown—
gold, pure gold, was needed. If the dwarfs could not get enough
gold, *she* would find some on earth and send it to that most skillful
dwarf.

Then the beautiful goddess put on her traveling robes and swept   14
down the rainbow bridge. She walked for miles and miles over the
earth in search of gold for her necklace. There was a gold ring here.
There was a gold bracelet there. But they belonged to the men and
women of the earth, whom Frigga loved as though they were her own
children. She did not wish to take such things from them. Besides it
would take many, many rings and bracelets to make enough gold.

At last she came to a statue that stood in a little village. It was   15
much taller than any man of the earth. It shone so brightly that beams
of light came from it and threw a dazzling glow for miles around. It
was made of pure gold.

Frigga cried out with pleasure! Here at last was more than enough   16
gold for her necklace. Just a small piece of the statue would be plenty.
As the queen of the gods came closer, she saw it was a statue of her
husband, Odin. It looked so much like Odin that for a minute she
expected it to speak. She would not have been surprised if it had
asked her what she was doing so far from her throne in Asgard.

But, no, it was only a dumb statue. She would just break off a   17
piece of gold big enough for the necklace and no one would miss it. If
it were missed, no one would know where it had gone. The dwarf
would have already made it into a beautiful necklace for her.

The men and women of the earth had made this statue of the All-   18
father so that they might worship him. Odin had been very pleased.
He had been kind to those faithful men and women, and had protected
them from the evil of the frost giants. In the dark of the night he often
walked through the village and smiled upon the simple homes full of
sleeping men and women. Even in the dark the gold statue glowed
and threw a warm light upon the stones of the street.

It was on such a night that Odin discovered a piece of gold had   19
been taken from his statue. He was very angry!

"What is this?" he shouted. "Who has dared to steal gold from my   20
statue? He shall pay heavily for this. Do not think I am unable to discover the thief!"

Odin's voice rang through the silent village. Dark clouds rolled   21
across the night sky. A fierce wind howled and tugged at the roofs of
the little houses. And the men, women and children pulled their blan-
kets over their heads and trembled with fear.

"The thief shall pay for this!" Odin roared again. The wind picked   22
up his words and howled, "Thief! Thief!" And the giants in the dark
cold depths of the earth laughed and shook their fists with joy. Evil
was again in the world and the great Odin was angry.

Now the most skillful dwarf had already turned the stolen piece   23
of gold into a necklace for Frigga. Never had there been such a handsome necklace. It had been hammered and twisted and carved in a
way that immediately caught everyone's attention. All the goddesses
gazed upon it with envy and wonder. Even Odin praised it.

"It is a thing of rare beauty," he had said. "Fit only for my queen   24
to wear." And he had smiled upon Frigga and she was very happy.

But now Odin did not smile. He did not seem to notice Frigga or   25
what she wore. He spoke seldom and sat upon his throne scowling
down upon the earth. Nothing Frigga said or did could rouse him. She
began to be afraid. What would happen if he ever found out she had
stolen the gold?

Finally Odin went back to the statue. He wrote magic verses upon   26
it so that the next morning it would be able to speak and name the
thief.

When Frigga saw him writing upon the statue from her throne in   27
Asgard, her face went white with terror. What could she do? Odin
might never forgive her. Should she confess? No. His anger would be
too terrible to bear. He must never know the truth. But how could she
stop him from finding out?

Quickly, while Odin was still down on the earth, Frigga fled to   28
the land of the dwarfs. Down the dark, winding underground passages
she stumbled. Loose stones slipped under her feet and several times
she almost fell. Down and down she went until she came to the workshop of the blackest dwarf. The most skillful dwarf could not help her
this time. The blackest dwarf must do the daring deed.

"Help me! Help me!" she begged as the tears ran down her pale 29
cheeks. The little dwarf gazed at her in surprise. His face was grimy
and red from working. His little green eyes gleamed with cunning.
But his heart softened as he looked at the frightened goddess.

"What can I do?" he croaked. "I have no power against the great 30
Odin."

"You must think of something," sobbed Frigga. "The statue will 31
speak my name in the morning. Break the statue! You must break the
statue!"

"I wouldn't dare," said the dwarf. 32

"Please! Please!" begged the goddess. And the great queen smiled 33
through her tears upon the little black dwarf. "You are the only living
creature who can help me. Is your heart hard and cold like the frost
giants'? Will you leave me to face my husband's fearful rage, when
by using your great cunning you can save me? Tell me you are not so
cruel! Please destroy the statue!" Again Frigga wept.

"Well," said the blackest dwarf slowly, "perhaps I can help you. I 34
would not do such a thing for anyone else. I shall be taking a great
chance."

"Surely you are not afraid to take a chance," Frigga said. She 35
smiled at him and the rosy color came back into her cheeks. "I shall
never forget your great kindness." Then she ran back up the dark passages and on up to her throne in Asgard.

The next morning Odin returned to the statue. Alas! It was broken 36
into a million gold pieces scattered upon the ground. There was no
longer any statue to speak the name of the thief. Odin stood looking
down at the heap of gold with his one blue eye. As Frigga watched
him from her throne, her heart stood still with fear. But Odin only
stood there silently thinking. She could not see the black rage that
darkened his brow, for his head was bent.

What was he thinking? Had he guessed now who the thief was? 37
But how could he? What was he doing—standing there?

And then the great king of the gods turned on his heel. He did not 38
look back. Without looking to the right or to the left he walked
straight ahead until he disappeared from sight.

Days passed. Weeks passed. Months passed. Odin did not return. 39
Frigga sat alone on her high throne. The frost giants laughed with

glee. Now who would rule the world and protect the people from evil? They blew cold blasts upon the earth. Storms raged on land and sea. The sun no longer warmed the world. Ice and snow covered everything.

In Asgard all was confusion and sadness. Odin had left the world. 40 His silent anger was worse than any rage Frigga or the other gods and goddesses had ever known.

Frigga remembered the happy days before she had risked so much 41 for the sake of vanity. The necklace no longer seemed beautiful. Because of it she had brought on all this evil and trouble. She knew that Odin had left the world because evil had been done, even though he might not have learned the name of the thief. She wept and prayed all night and all day for his forgiveness.

Then one day, when they had given up hope of ever seeing Odin 42 again, the great All-father returned. He smiled upon Frigga and the other gods and goddesses. He looked down upon the dark, cold world. And, as he gazed, the ice began to melt. The sun began to break through the gray clouds. The plants began to grow. Odin was no longer angry. All was forgiven. The frost giants grumbled and growled, but there was nothing they could do.

Frigga never knew whether Odin had guessed the whole truth, but 43 she never wore the beautiful gold necklace again.

Focusing on the Story

1. Describe Frigga. What did she look like, and what was her character like?
2. One day Frigga decided she wanted a new necklace for her new gown. Why did she feel she had to have such a special necklace?
3. Frigga sent a messenger to a skillful blacksmith to make the necklace, but there was a problem. What was the problem?
4. On her journey across the earth, Frigga finally came to a large statue that stood in a village. What did Frigga take from the statue? How did her husband Odin feel when he discovered the theft?
5. Why did Frigga ask one of the dwarfs to destroy the statue?
6. Who represents goodness in the story? Who represents evil?

Interpreting and Evaluating

1. Frigga has both positive and negative qualities. List some positive qualities, as well as several negative ones.
2. Because of the necklace, Frigga faces both external and internal conflicts. What are they and how does she resolve them?
3. How does Frigga persuade the dwarf to destroy the statue? Why does the dwarf agree to do it?
4. Name some common persuasion techniques used today. How are they similar or different to the way Frigga appeals to the dwarf to break the statue?
5. A small thing can lead to a heap of trouble. How does Frigga's seemingly innocent desire cause evil to enter the world?

Ideas for Writing and Further Discussion

1. Why did Frigga feel compelled to hide the truth from Odin? Write a paragraph in which you discuss two or three reasons why Frigga decided not to tell Odin about the theft.
2. Has a small event in your life ever caused you big trouble? You may, for example, have told a seemingly harmless lie and before you knew it, you were in a big mess. Think about a time when a seemingly small event developed into a big problem and write a paragraph or two about it. Start by describing the event and show how it escalated into a big problem.

Three Strong Women

❖

Retold by Claus Stamm

About the Author

Claus Stamm has lived in Japan, where he heard this story and decided to retell it in English. He has also written *The Very Special Badgers: A Tale of Magic from Japan.*

 Something to Think About

Wrestling has long been a popular sport in Japan. Is strength measured only by physical force?

Words to Keep in Mind

furrow *(20)* deep, narrow groove in the ground as made by a plow

rheumatism *(52)* condition characterized by inflammation or pain in muscle, joints, or fibrous tissue

chortle *(57)* laugh softly with a deep voice; chuckle

waggle *(87)* move back and forth; wag

Long ago, in Japan, there lived a famous wrestler, and he was on his way to the capital city to wrestle before the Emperor. 1

He strode down the road on legs thick as the trunks of small trees.   2
He had been walking for seven hours and could, and probably would,
walk for seven more without getting tired.

The time was autumn, the sky was a cold, watery blue, the air   3
chilly. In the small bright sun, the trees along the roadside glowed red
and orange.

The wrestler hummed to himself, "Zun-zun-zun," in time with the   4
long swing of his legs. Wind blew through his thin brown robe, and
he wore no sword at his side. He felt proud that he needed no sword,
even in the darkest and loneliest places. The icy air on his body only
reminded him that few tailors would have been able to make expensive warm clothes for a man so broad and tall. He felt much as a
wrestler should—strong, healthy, and rather conceited.

A soft roar of fast-moving water beyond the trees told him that he   5
was passing above a river bank. He "zun-zunned" louder; he loved
the sound of his voice and wanted it to sound clearly above the rushing water.

He thought: They call me Forever-Mountain because I am such a   6
good strong wrestler—big, too. I'm a fine, brave man and far too
modest ever to say so. . . .

Just then he saw a girl who must have come up from the river, for   7
she steadied a bucket on her head.

Her hands on the bucket were small, and there was a dimple on   8
each thumb, just below the knuckle. She was a round little girl with
red cheeks and a nose like a friendly button. Her eyes looked as
though she were thinking of ten thousand funny stories at once. She
clambered up onto the road and walked ahead of the wrestler, jolly
and bounceful.

"If I don't tickle that fat girl, I shall regret it all my life," said the   9
wrestler under his breath. "She's sure to go 'squeak' and I shall laugh
and laugh. If she drops her bucket, that will be even funnier—and I
can always run and fill it again and even carry it home for her."

He tiptoed up and poked her lightly in the ribs with one huge finger.   10

"Kochokochokocho!" he said, a fine, ticklish sound in Japanese.   11

The girl gave a satisfying squeal, giggled, and brought one arm   12
down so that the wrestler's hand was caught between it and her body.

"Ho-ho-ho! You've caught me! I can't move at all!" said the 13
wrestler, laughing.

"I know," said the jolly girl. 14

He felt that it was very good-tempered of her to take a joke so 15
well, and started to pull his hand free.

Somehow, he could not. 16

He tried again, using a little more strength. 17

"Now, now—let me go, little girl," he said. "I am a very powerful 18
man. If I pull too hard I might hurt you."

"Pull," said the girl. "I admire powerful men." 19

She began to walk, and though the wrestler tugged and pulled 20
until his feet dug great furrows in the ground, he had to follow. She
couldn't have paid him less attention if he had been a puppy—a small
one.

Ten minutes later, still tugging while trudging helplessly after her, 21
he was glad that the road was lonely and no one was there to see.

"Please let me go," he pleaded. "I am the famous wrestler 22
Forever-Mountain. I must go and show my strength before the
Emperor"—he burst out weeping from shame and confusion—"and
you're hurting my hand!"

The girl steadied the bucket on her head with her free hand and 23
dimpled sympathetically over her shoulder. "You poor, sweet little
Forever-Mountain," she said. "Are you tired? Shall I carry you? I can
leave the water here and come back for it later."

"I do not want you to carry me. I want you to let me go, and then I 24
want to forget I ever saw you. What do you want with me?" moaned
the pitiful wrestler.

"I only want to help you," said the girl, now pulling him steadily 25
up and up a narrow mountain path. "Oh, I am sure you'll have no
more trouble than anyone else when you come up against the other
wrestlers. You'll win, or else you'll lose, and you won't be too badly
hurt either way. But aren't you afraid you might meet a really *strong*
man someday?"

Forever-Mountain turned white. He stumbled. He was imagining 26
being laughed at throughout Japan as "Hardly-Ever-Mountain."

She glanced back. 27

"You see? Tired already," she said. "I'll walk more slowly. Why   28
don't you come along to my mother's house and let us make a strong
man of you? The wrestling in the capital isn't due to begin for three
months. I know, because Grandmother thought she'd go. You'd be
spending all that time in bad company and wasting what little power
you have."

"All right. Three months. I'll come along," said the wrestler. He   29
felt he had nothing more to lose. Also, he feared that the girl might
become angry if he refused, and place him in the top of a tree until he
changed his mind.

"Fine," she said happily. "We are almost there."   30

She freed his hand. It had become red and a little swollen. "But if   31
you break your promise and run off, I shall have to chase you and
carry you back."

Soon they arrived in a small valley. A simple farmhouse with a   32
thatched roof stood in the middle.

"Grandmother is at home, but she is an old lady and she's proba-   33
bly sleeping." The girl shaded her eyes with one hand. "But Mother
should be bringing our cow back from the field—oh, there's Mother
now!"

She waved. The woman coming around the corner of the house   34
put down the cow she was carrying and waved back.

She smiled and came across the grass, walking with a lively   35
bounce like her daughter's. Well, maybe her bounce was a little more
solid, thought the wrestler.

"Excuse me," she said, brushing some cow hair from her dress   36
and dimpling, also like her daughter. "These mountain paths are full
of stones. They hurt the cow's feet. And who is the nice young man
you've brought, Maru-me?"

The girl explained. "And we have only three months!" she fin-   37
ished anxiously.

"Well, it's not long enough to do much, but it's not so short a time   38
that we can't do something," said her mother, looking thoughtful.
"But he does look terribly feeble. He'll need a lot of good things to
eat. Maybe when he gets stronger he can help Grandmother with
some of the easy work about the house."

"That will be fine!" said the girl, and she called her grand- 39
mother—loudly, for the old lady was a little deaf.

"I'm coming!" came a creaky voice from inside the house, and a 40
little old woman leaning on a stick and looking very sleepy tottered
out of the door. As she came toward them she stumbled over the roots
of a great oak tree.

"Heh! My eyes aren't what they used to be. That's the fourth time 41
this month I've stumbled over that tree," she complained and, wrapping her skinny arms about its trunk, pulled it out of the ground.

"Oh, Grandmother! You should have let me pull it up for you," 42
said Maru-me.

"Hm. I hope I didn't hurt my poor old back," muttered the old 43
lady. She called out, "Daughter! Throw that tree away like a good
girl, so no one will fall over it. But make sure it doesn't hit anybody."

"You can help Mother with the tree," Maru-me said to Forever- 44
Mountain. "On second thought, you'd better not help. Just watch."

Her mother went to the tree, picked it up in her two hands, and 45
threw it—clumsily and with a little gasp, the way a woman throws.
Up went the tree, sailing end over end, growing smaller and smaller
as it flew. It landed with a faint crash far up the mountainside.

"Ah, how clumsy," she said. "I meant to throw it *over* the moun- 46
tain. It's probably blocking the path now, and I'll have to get up early
tomorrow to move it."

The wrestler was not listening. He had very quietly fainted. 47

"Oh! We must put him to bed," said Maru-me. 48

"Poor, feeble young man," said her mother. 49

"I hope we can do something for him. Here, let me carry him, he's 50
light," said the grandmother. She slung him over her shoulder and
carried him into the house, creaking along with her cane.

The next day they began the work of making Forever-Mountain 51
over into what they thought a strong man should be. They gave him
the simplest food to eat, and the toughest. Day by day they prepared
his rice with less and less water, until no ordinary man could have
chewed or digested it.

Every day he was made to do the work of five men, and every 52
evening he wrestled with Grandmother. Maru-me and her mother

agreed that Grandmother, being old and feeble, was the least likely to injure him accidentally. They hoped the exercise might be good for the old lady's rheumatism.

He grew stronger and stronger but was hardly aware of it. 53
Grandmother could still throw him easily into the air—and catch him again—without ever changing her sweet old smile.

He quite forgot that outside this valley he was one of the greatest 54
wrestlers in Japan and was called Forever-Mountain. His legs had been like logs; now they were like pillars. His big hands were hard as stones, and when he cracked his knuckles the sound was like trees splitting on a cold night.

Sometimes he did an exercise that wrestlers do in Japan—raising 55
one foot high above the ground and bringing it down with a crash. Then people in nearby villages looked up at the winter sky and told one another that it was very late in the year for thunder.

Soon he could pull up a tree as well as the grandmother. He could 56
even throw one—but only a small distance. One evening, near the end of his third month, he wrestled with Grandmother and held her down for half a minute.

"Heh-heh!" She chortled and got up, smiling with every wrinkle. 57
"I would never have believed it!"

Maru-me squealed with joy and threw her arms around him— 58
gently, for she was afraid of cracking his ribs.

"Very good, very good! What a strong man," said her mother, 59
who had just come home from the fields, carrying, as usual, the cow. She put the cow down and patted the wrestler on the back.

They agreed that he was now ready to show some *real* strength 60
before the Emperor.

"Take the cow along with you tomorrow when you go," said the 61
mother. "Sell her and buy yourself a belt—a silken belt. Buy the fattest and heaviest one you can find. Wear it when you appear before the Emperor, as a souvenir from us."

"I wouldn't think of taking your only cow. You've already done 62
too much for me. And you'll need her to plow the fields, won't you?"

They burst out laughing. Maru-me squealed, her mother roared. 63
The grandmother cackled so hard and long that she choked and had to
be pounded on the back.

"Oh, dear," said the mother, still laughing. "You didn't think we 64
used our cow for anything like *work!* Why, Grandmother here is
stronger than five cows!"

"The cow is our pet." Maru-me giggled. "She has lovely brown 65
eyes."

"But it really gets tiresome having to carry her back and forth 66
each day so that she has enough grass to eat," said her mother.

"Then you must let me give you all the prize money that I win," 67
said Forever-Mountain.

"Oh, no! We wouldn't think of it!" said Maru-me. "Because we 68
all like you too much to sell you anything. And it is not proper to
accept gifts of money from strangers."

"True," said Forever-Mountain. "I will now ask your mother's 69
and grandmother's permission to marry you. I want to be one of the
family."

"Oh! I'll get a wedding dress ready!" said Maru-me. 70

The mother and grandmother pretended to consider very seri- 71
ously, but they quickly agreed.

Next morning Forever-Mountain tied his hair up in the topknot 72
that all Japanese wrestlers wear, and got ready to leave. He thanked
Maru-me and her mother and bowed very low to the grandmother,
since she was the oldest and had been a fine wrestling partner.

Then he picked up the cow in his arms and trudged up the moun- 73
tain. When he reached the top, he slung the cow over one shoulder
and waved good-by to Maru-me.

At the first town he came to, Forever-Mountain sold the cow. She 74
brought a good price because she was unusually fat from never having worked in her life. With the money, he bought the heaviest silken
belt he could find.

When he reached the palace grounds, many of the other wrestlers 75
were already there, sitting about, eating enormous bowls of rice,
comparing one another's weight and telling stories. They paid little

attention to Forever-Mountain, except to wonder why he had arrived so late this year. Some of them noticed that he had grown very quiet and took no part at all in their boasting.

All the ladies and gentlemen of the court were waiting in a spe-   76
cial courtyard for the wrestling to begin. They wore many robes, one on top of another, heavy with embroidery and gold cloth, and sweat ran down their faces and froze in the winter afternoon. The gentlemen had long swords so weighted with gold and precious stones that they could never have used them, even if they had known how. The court ladies, with their long black hair hanging down behind, had their faces painted dead white, which made them look frightened. They had pulled out their real eyebrows and painted new ones high above the place where eyebrows are supposed to be, and this made them all look as though they were very surprised at something.

Behind a screen sat the Emperor—by himself, because he was too   77
noble for ordinary people to look at. He was a lonely old man with a kind, tired face. He hoped the wrestling would end quickly so that he could go to his room and write poems.

The first two wrestlers chosen to fight were Forever-Mountain   78
and a wrestler who was said to have the biggest stomach in the country. He and Forever-Mountain both threw some salt into the ring. It was understood that this drove away evil spirits.

Then the other wrestler, moving his stomach somewhat out of the   79
way, raised his foot and brought it down with a fearful stamp. He glared fiercely at Forever-Mountain as if to say, "Now *you* stamp, you poor frightened man!"

Forever-Mountain raised his foot. He brought it down.   80

There was a sound like thunder, the earth shook, and the other   81
wrestler bounced into the air and out of the ring, as gracefully as any soap bubble.

He picked himself up and bowed to the Emperor's screen.   82

"The earth-god is angry. Possibly there is something the matter   83
with the salt," he said. "I do not think I shall wrestle this season." And he walked out, looking very suspiciously over one shoulder at Forever-Mountain.

Five other wrestlers then and there decided that they were not 84
wrestling this season, either. They all looked annoyed with Forever-
Mountain.

From then on, Forever-Mountain brought his foot down lightly. 85
As each wrestler came into the ring, he picked him up very gently,
carried him out, and placed him before the Emperor's screen, bowing
most courteously every time.

The court ladies' eyebrows went up even higher. The gentlemen 86
looked disturbed and a little afraid. They loved to see fierce, strong
men tugging and grunting at each other, but Forever-Mountain was a
little too much for them. Only the Emperor was happy behind his
screen, for now, with the wrestling over so quickly, he would have
that much more time to write his poems. He ordered all the prize
money handed over to Forever-Mountain.

"But," he said, "you had better not wrestle any more." He stuck a 87
finger through his screen and waggled it at the other wrestlers, who
were sitting on the ground weeping with disappointment like great fat
babies.

Forever-Mountain promised not to wrestle any more. Everybody 88
looked relieved. The wrestlers sitting on the ground almost smiled.

"I think I shall become a farmer," Forever-Mountain said, and left 89
at once to go back to Maru-me.

Maru-me was waiting for him. When she saw him coming, she ran 90
down the mountain, picked him up, together with the heavy bags of
prize money, and carried him halfway up the mountainside. Then she
giggled and put him down. The rest of the way she let him carry her.

Forever-Mountain kept his promise to the Emperor and never 91
fought in public again. His name was forgotten in the capital. But up
in the mountains, sometimes, the earth shakes and rumbles, and they
say that is Forever-Mountain and Maru-me's grandmother practicing
wrestling in the hidden valley.

Focusing on the Story

1. Where is Forever-Mountain, the famous wrestler, going one fine autumn day?
2. At the beginning of the story, Forever-Mountain says of himself, "I'm a fine, brave man and far too modest to ever say so . . . ." What is ironic about this statement? Is he really modest?
3. Who does he meet as he is "passing above a river bank"?
4. Who are the women that Forever-Mountain meets at the simple farmhouse?
5. Why don't the three women boast about their strength? Is their strength physical only? What must Forever-Mountain do to become stronger?

Interpreting and Evaluating

1. While pulling the wrestler up the mountain path, Maru-me says, "You'll win or else you'll lose, and you won't be too badly hurt either way." What does she mean by this statement?
2. While he is with the three women in the valley, he grows stronger and stronger, yet he isn't aware of it. Why isn't he so aware of his strength now?
3. Why doesn't Forever-Mountain take part in the other wrestlers' boasting before the wrestling contest at the Imperial Court begins? What has he learned from the three women?
4. At the end of the story, Forever-Mountain promises to forget about wrestling and decides to become a farmer. How can he make this promise so easily now? How has his attitude changed?
5. After the wrestling is over, the other wrestlers are "sitting on the ground weeping with disappointment like great fat babies." How is their reaction similar to Forever-Mountain's after Maru-me has hurt his hand? What has Forever-Mountain taught the other wrestlers?
6. Humor often depends on the unexpected. What are some unexpected situations that are funny in the story?
7. What does this story reveal about Japanese society? What qualities do the Japanese admire? What qualities do they dislike?

An Idea for Writing and Further Discussion

Humorous stories are often based on unusual characters that solve problems in unexpected and ridiculous ways. Write a humorous story of your own. Begin by choosing a problem and think of a ridiculous solution. The setting may be real or imaginary. Tell the events in chronological order.

Race,
Culture,
and
Identity

✛

A Boy with His Hat over His Crotch

❖

Gish Jen

About the Author

Gish Jen lives in Massachusetts and writes about contemporary Chinese immigrant experiences. "A Boy with His Hat over His Crotch" is taken from her novel *Typical American.*

Something to Think About

What is it like to come to this country as a foreign student? What is it like to go to another country to live and study? What problems might arise? How could misunderstandings occur?

Words to Keep in Mind

orotund *(1)* pompous; self-important

dimpled *(1)* with small indentations or impressions as from smiling

placid *(1)* peaceful; unmoving

waxing and waning *(1)* increasing and decreasing in intensity

burial mound *(19)* pile of earth to form a rounded hill over a grave site

Confucius *(19)* Chinese philosopher, ca. 500 B.C., whose teachings became the basis for one of China's major religions

sanguine *(22)* confident; hopeful

dispensed with *(22)* got along without

puckered *(22)* contracted

carnivorous *(34)* meat-eating

permeable *(42)* porous; easy to pass through

shui jiao *(43)* making dumplings (Mandarin Chinese)

crescendo *(52)* gradual increase of intensity of music

P icture him. Young, orotund. Longish hair managed with grease. A   1
new, light gray, too dressy, double-breasted suit made him look even
shorter than his five feet three and three-quarter inches. Otherwise he
was himself—large-faced, dimpled, with eyebrows that rode nervously up and up, away from his flat, wide, placid nose. He had small
teeth set in vast expanses of gum; those round ears; and delicate,
almost maidenly skin that tended to flush and pale with the waxing
and waning of his digestive problems. Everywhere he went, he carried a Panama hat with him, though he never put it on, and it was
always in his way; he seemed to have picked up an idea about gentlemen, or hats—something—that was proving hard to let go.

In sum, he was a doll, and the Foreign Student Affairs secretary,   2
though she loathed her job, loathed her boss, loathed *working,* liked
him.

"Name?" he repeated, or rather "nem," which he knew to be   3
wrong. He turned red, thinking of his trouble with long a's, th's, l's,
consonants at the ends of words. Was it beneath a scholar to hate the
alphabet? Anyway, he did.

"Naaame," she said, writing it down. She'd seen this before, for-   4
eign students who could read and write and speak a little, but who just
couldn't get the conversation. N-A-M-E.

"Name Y. F. Chang." (His surname as he pronounced it then   5
sounded like the beginning of *angst;* it would be years before he was
used to hearing Chang rhyme with *twang.*)

"Eng-lish-name," said Cammy. E-N-G-L-I-S-H-N-A-M-E.   6

"I Chin-ese," he said, and was about to explain that Y. F. were his 7
initials when she laughed.

"Eng-lish-name," she said again. 8

"What you laughing?" 9

Later he realized this to be a very daring thing to ask, that he 10
never would have asked a Chinese girl why she was laughing. But
then, a Chinese girl never would have been laughing, not like that.
Not a nice Chinese girl, anyway. What a country he was in!

"I'm laughing at you." Her voice rang, playful yet deeper than he 11
would have expected. She smelled of perfume. He could not begin to
guess her age. "At *you!*"

"Me?" With mock offense, he drew his chin back. 12

"You," she said again. "Me?" "You." "Me?" They were joking! In 13
English! *Shuo de chu*—he spoke, and the words came out! *Ting de
dong*—he listened and understood!

"English name," she said again, finally. She showed him her type- 14
writer, the form she had to fill out.

"No English name." How to say initials? He was sorry to disap- 15
point her. Then he brightened. "You give me."

"*I*-give-you-a-name?" 16

"Sure. You give." There was something about speaking English 17
that carried him away.

"I'll-hang-onto-this-form-overnight," she tried to tell him. "That 18
- way - you - find - a - name - you - like - better - you - can - tell - me
- tomorrow."

Too much, he didn't get it. Anyway, he waited, staring—exercis- 19
ing the outsider's privilege, to be rude. How colorful she was! Orange
hair, pink face, blue eyes. Red nails. Green dress. And under the
dress, breasts large and solid as earthworks. He thought of the burial
mounds that dotted the Chinese countryside—the small mounds for
nobodies, the big mounds for big shots. This woman put him in mind
of the biggest mound he had ever seen: in Shandong, that was,
Confucius's grave.

Meanwhile, she ran through her ex-beaux. Robert? Eugene? 20
Norman? She toyed with a stray curl. Fred? John? Steve? Ken?
"Ralph," she said finally. She wrote it down. R-A-L-P-H. "Do you
like it?"

"Sure!" He beamed.   21

Walking home, though, *Ralph* was less sanguine. Had he been too   22
hasty? He did this, he knew; he dispensed with things, trying to be
like other people—decisive, practical—only to discover he'd over-
done it. His stomach puckered with anxiety. And sure enough, when
he asked around later he found that the other Chinese students (there
were five of them in the master's degree program) had all stuck with
their initials, or picked names for themselves, carefully, or else had
wise people help them.

"Ralph," said smooth-faced Old Chao (Old Something-or-another   23
being what younger classmates called older classmates, who in turn
called them Little Something-or-another). He looked it up in a book
he had. "Means *wolf*," he said, then looked that up in a dictionary. "*A
kind of dog*," he translated.

A kind of dog, thought Ralph.   24

For himself, Old Chao had Henry, which turned out to be the   25
name of at least eight kings. "*My father picked it for me*," he said.

It would have been better if Ralph sounded a bit more like Yifeng;   26
in the art of picking English names (which everyone seemed to know
except him), that was considered desirable. But so what? And who
cared what it meant? Ralph decided that what was on the form didn't
matter. He was a man with a mission; what mattered was that he reg-
ister for the right courses, that he attend the right classes, that he buy
the right books. All of this proved more difficult than he'd antici-
pated. He discovered, for instance, that he wasn't on the class list for
two of his courses, and that for one of them, enrollment was already
closed. To address these problems, he did what he did when his
tuition didn't arrive, and when his other two classes turned out to
meet at the same time: he found his way to the Foreign Student
Affairs Office, where gaily colored Cammy would help him.

Ralph had noticed by then that she was pretty, or figured she must   27
be, as about half the men with affairs to discuss with her didn't seem
to be foreign students. ("Fan club," explained Old Chao, idiom book
in hand.) With her big barbarian frame and long nose and hairy fore-
arms, though, she just wasn't Ralph's type (the hair bothered him
especially—like a monkey's, he thought); and anyway, he was too

exhausted to be thinking about such things—having come, he belat-edly realized, to the complete other side of the world. Mile after mile, he'd travelled, *li* after *li*, by boat and by train, only to have to get him-self going. His degree, his degree!

And so to Cammy he was grateful, nothing more.   28

"Tank you," he said. "Tank you." One day he helped fix her pen- 29 cil sharpener, and when she said "Tank *you*," he answered, "Sure!" And after that, whenever he said "Tank you," she answered "Sure!" too. This came with a wink, and a kind of sideways look that made Ralph's pants bulge—lucky thing he was still carrying that hat around.

Did he confuse this phenomenon with love? Not yet. He stacked 30 paper for Cammy. He taught her to say thank you in Chinese. "Shay shay!" she said now, whenever she saw him, whether she had reason to thank him or not. "Shay shay shay shay!" Ralph tried to get her to speak more correctly. "Sh-yeh," he told her. "Sh-yeh, sh-yeh." He con-centrated on getting his own pronunciation right, not wanting to pass on to her his Shanghainese hiss. So little of what he knew counted here; he offered what he could on a kind of tray. "Isn't that what I said?" she asked. "Shay shay?" And before he'd had a chance to say yes or no, she was back to "Shay shay shay shay!" again, with such exuberance, Ralph didn't have the heart to do anything but nod. "Good!"

"You know, one of these days I'm going to study Chinese," said 31 Cammy. "Chinese or French. Or else ballet, I've always loved ballet."

"Ah," said Ralph (this being the sort of thing he was beginning to 32 understand he should say instead of "Wha?" when there was some-thing he couldn't catch).

More favors, innocent enough—packages to the mailbox, expedi- 33 tious disposal of a bumblebee. And, of course, help with her boss, Mr. Fitt.

Now Mr. Fitt was a grim man, an enforcer, with a small, sneering 34 mouth; in another life he might have been a carnivorous fish. In this life, he carried a rolled-up newspaper in his thick hand like a bat he meant to use on someone. When Ralph wandered onto the scene, Mr. Fitt was tapping that bat on his thigh; his other hand was all five hairy fingers on Cammy's neat desk.

"But I w-was here. At one on th-the b-b-button." The sound of   35
Cammy choked up made Ralph's throat catch. "Wasn't I, Ralph?
Wasn't I?"

Ralph gave solemn testimony. Mr. Fitt straightened up, glaring.   36
Cammy was all shay shays. "Tell me how to say it again," she said. "I
know I don't say it right. I don't do anything right."

"No, no, you pronounce very good."   37

"No I don't. You say it again, the right way."   38

Ralph hesitated. "Shay shay."   39

"Shay shay." She lit up. "Shay shay! You mean, I *am* saying it   40
right? Shay shay?"

Ralph nodded, beamed, situated his hat.   41

More and more now, he was beginning to know what was what.   42
He was lonely still, but it was only a mist, a weather front that passed
through him when he was alone, a feeling of having turned too permeable. When he was working, he was fine. And having launched
into his work, he did not go to the Foreign Student Affairs Office anymore, but rather to the stone-stepped library, where he studied and
studied at the endless oak tables; or else to the kitchen at the end of
the hall in his rooming house on 123rd Street. There, on the blackboard by the stove, he puzzled out problems with his classmates.
Between equations, they marvelled that their tests would be scored to
the whole point, instead of to five decimal places. Was it fair? Who
knew? This was America. They forged on, mostly speaking
Mandarin, saving their English for impersonations of certain profes-
sors.

The kitchen was where Ralph spent his free time too, learning to   43
cook. He could make three dishes now—boiled rice, egg rice, and
fried eggs. Having thrown several successful *shui jiao*-making parties, his classmates were organizing a cooperative cooking program,
and Ralph was practicing up, to be sure he'd be able to participate.
Other developments: he'd discovered supper for a dollar at General
Lee's, and also banana splits with extra nuts and marshmallow sauce
(the specialty of the luncheonette down the street). Also, he'd bought
a lamp for his room, from the secondhand store next to the grocery he
used to go to. Already he had a history in America. Now he went to a
new, cheaper grocery, even though the first grocer was friendlier than

the second, and had been so nice as to count his change out slowly, one coin at a time.

From his doorway, the first grocer scowled at him.   44

The problem sets got harder.   45

His lamp turned out to have a short in it.   46

His problem sets started to come back red.   47

More red.   48

Who had ever thought the rice barrel could become an engineer?   49

New York lost its gleam. He drifted through its streets as if   50
through an exhausted, dusty land, no detail of which had changed in a
thousand years.

Then he remembered a form he was supposed to have handed in   51
(some form, he had always been bad at that sort of thing) and, stopping into the Foreign Student Affairs Office, discovered Cammy
arguing once again with Mr. Fitt. What a bully that man was! His
whole long belly overhung Cammy's desk; he had his arms spread
and bent, his fingers on her blotter. Cammy was holding her hands
over her ears.

Ralph's heart rumbled like a Peking Opera drum; it was the   52
crescendo before—*crash of the cymbals!*—a hero appeared.

Focusing on the Story

1. Describe Yifeng Chang as he arrives at the Foreign Student Affairs Office.

2. Describe Cammy, the Foreign Student Affairs Office secretary, as Yifeng Chang sees her. What are some things Cammy does for Yifeng Chang? How does she make him feel? What are some things Yifeng does for Cammy? Why can Yifeng not "begin to guess her age"? How does Cammy differ from young Chinese women?

3. What does Yifeng's American name Ralph mean? How does Yifeng feel about his new name when he discovers its meaning?

4. Yifeng accepts his new name rather quickly, without thinking it over. How does he later justify his rash behavior?

5. What is Yifeng or Ralph's "mission" in the United States? Why can't he accomplish this mission in China?

Interpreting and Evaluating

1. It has been customary for new immigrants to this country to anglicize their names for ease of pronunciation and spelling by native speakers of English. How much of your identity does your name represent? How would you feel if someone decided to change your name by whim?
2. When Yifeng realizes that he has accepted his new name too readily, he rationalizes that his hasty move is not important. What does his behavior say about his character?
3. Ralph studies at the library, finds where the best bargains are, and learns to cook. What does all this, as well as his other actions, say about Ralph's ability to adapt? Will he ultimately succeed? Explain.
4. At the end of the story, Ralph comes to Cammy's rescue again—"a hero appeared." Based on evidence in the story, what predictions can you make about Cammy and Ralph's future relationship? Could their relationship develop into a romantic one? Explain.
5. How may a marriage between people from different cultures be more difficult than a marriage between people from similar backgrounds?

Ideas for Writing and Further Discussion

1. What are some causes of misunderstandings between people from different cultures? Write an essay in which you explore several causes of misunderstandings between people from different cultures. Suggested *thesis*: two or three such causes.
   Each *body paragraph* should discuss one cause. You may suggest a solution to the problem in your conclusion.
2. Although Yifeng, or Ralph, has many obstacles to overcome, most people would probably agree that he has what it takes to succeed in this country. Analyze Ralph's character. What in his character will help him succeed? Write an essay in which you discuss several of Ralph's qualities that will contribute to his success in his new country. Suggested *thesis*: three or four such qualities.
   Each *body paragraph* should explore one quality and give examples from the story to illustrate the quality and show how possessing such a quality will lead to success. Or one body paragraph may discuss some obstacles Yifeng, or Ralph, has to overcome; the remaining body paragraphs should explore his positive qualities.

By Any Other Name

❖

Santha Rama Rau

About the Author

Santha Rama Rau was born in India in 1923, but received her education in the West. Because of her familiarity with both Eastern and Western points of view, her books are highly regarded for their insight. This selection is taken from her autobiography, *Gifts of Passage.*

Something to Think About

India was ruled by Great Britain from the 1700s to 1947. What effects may a ruling country have on a local culture? What kinds of stereotypes may be formed? What effects of Great Britain's rule over the American Colonies can you see today in your own life?

Words to Keep in Mind

precarious *(3)* not secure; unstable

baffled *(3)* frustrated; confused

insular *(6)* isolated; separated

Lord Krishna *(6)* ancient Hindu god whose childhood pranks provide popular stories for Indian children even today

veranda *(7)* porch

kohl *(9)* special coal used as eye makeup in India and many other countries

palpitating *(15)* trembling, throbbing

207

incomprehensible *(15)* impossible to understand

chapatties *(16)* whole-grain bread made without baking powder or yeast

ayah *(18)* Indian maid (literally *grandmother*)

sedately *(22)* calmly

tonga *(34)* a light two-wheeled wagon common in India

peevishness *(34)* irritation

At the Anglo-Indian day school in Zorinabad to which my sister   1
and I were sent when she was eight and I was five and a half, they
changed our names. On the first day of school, a hot, windless morning of a north Indian September, we stood in the headmistress's study
and she said, "Now you're the *new* girls. What are your names?"

My sister answered for us. "I am Premila, and she"—nodding in   2
my direction—"is Santha."

The headmistress had been in India, I suppose, fifteen years or so,   3
but she still smiled her helpless inability to cope with Indian names.
Her rimless half-glasses glittered, and the precarious bun on the top
of her head trembled as she shook her head. "Oh, my dears, those are
much too hard for me. Suppose we give you pretty English names.
Wouldn't that be more jolly? Let's see, now—Pamela for you, I
think." She shrugged in a baffled way at my sister. "That's as close as
I can get. And for *you,*" she said to me, "how about Cynthia? Isn't that
nice?"

My sister was always less easily intimidated than I was, and   4
while she kept a stubborn silence, I said, "Thank you," in a very tiny
voice.

We had been sent to that school because my father, among his   5
responsibilities as an officer of the civil service, had a tour of duty to
perform in the villages around that steamy little provincial town,

where he had his headquarters at that time. He used to make his
shorter inspection tours on horseback, and a week before, in the stale
heat of a typically postmonsoon day, we had waved good-by to him
and a little procession—an assistant, a secretary, two bearers, and the
man to look after the bedding rolls and luggage. They rode away
through our large garden, still bright green from the rains, and we
turned back into the twilight of the house and the sound of fans whispering in every room.

Up to then, my mother had refused to send Premila to school in   6
the British-run establishments of that time, because, she used to say,
"you can bury a dog's tail for seven years and it still comes out curly,
and you can take a Britisher away from his home for a lifetime and he
still remains insular." The examinations and degrees from entirely
Indian schools were not, in those days, considered valid. In my case,
the question had never come up, and probably never would have
come up if Mother's extraordinary good health had not broken down.
For the first time in my life, she was not able to continue the lessons
she had been giving us every morning. So our Hindi books were put
away, the stories of the Lord Krishna as a little boy were left in midair, and we were sent to the Anglo-Indian school.

That first day at school is still, when I think of it, a remarkable   7
one. At that age, if one's name is changed, one develops a curious
form of dual personality. I remember having a certain detached and
disbelieving concern in the actions of "Cynthia," but certainly no
responsibility. Accordingly, I followed the thin, erect back of the
headmistress down the veranda to my classroom feeling, at most, a
passing interest in what was going to happen to me in this strange,
new atmosphere of School.

The building was Indian in design, with wide verandas opening   8
into a central courtyard, but Indian verandas are usually whitewashed, with stone floors. These, in the tradition of British schools,
were painted dark brown and had matting on the floors. It gave a feeling of extra intensity to the heat.

I suppose there were about a dozen Indian children in the   9
school—which contained perhaps forty children in all—and four of
them were in my class. They were all sitting at the back of the room,
and I went to join them. I sat next to a small solemn girl who didn't

smile at me. She had long, glossy-black braids and wore a cotton dress, but she still kept on her Indian jewelry—a gold chain around her neck, thin gold bracelets, and tiny ruby studs in her ears. Like most Indian children, she had a rim of black kohl around her eyes. The cotton dress should have looked strange, but all I could think of was that I should ask my mother if I couldn't wear a dress to school, too, instead of my Indian clothes.

I can't remember too much about the proceedings in class that 10 day, except for the beginning. The teacher pointed to me and asked me to stand up. "Now, dear, tell the class your name."

I said nothing. 11

"Come along," she said, frowning slightly. "What's your name, 12 dear?"

"I don't know," I said, finally. 13

The English children in the front of the class—there were about 14 eight or ten of them—giggled and twisted around in their chairs to look at me. I sat down quickly and opened my eyes very wide, hoping in that way to dry them off. The little girl with the braids put out her hand and very lightly touched my arm. She still didn't smile.

Most of that morning I was rather bored. I looked briefly at the 15 children's drawings pinned to the wall, and then concentrated on a lizard clinging to the ledge of the high, barred window behind the teacher's head. Occasionally it would shoot out its long yellow tongue for a fly, and then it would rest, with its eyes closed and its belly palpitating, as though it were swallowing several times quickly. The lessons were mostly concerned with reading and writing and simple numbers—things that my mother had already taught me—and I paid very little attention. The teacher wrote on the easel blackboard words like "bat" and "cat," which seemed babyish to me; only "apple" was new and incomprehensible.

When it was time for the lunch recess, I followed the girl with 16 braids out onto the veranda. There the children from the other classes were assembled. I saw Premila at once and ran over to her, as she had charge of our lunchbox. The children were all opening packages and sitting down to eat sandwiches. Premila and I were the only ones who had Indian food—thin wheat chapatties, some vegetable curry, and a bottle of buttermilk. Premila thrust half of it into my hand and whispered fiercely that I should go and sit with my class, because that was what the others seemed to be doing.

The enormous black eyes of the little Indian girl from my class looked at my food longingly, so I offered her some. But she only shook her head and plowed her way solemnly through her sandwiches.

I was very sleepy after lunch, because at home we always took a siesta. It was usually a pleasant time of day, with the bedroom darkened against the harsh afternoon sun, the drifting off into sleep with the sound of Mother's voice reading a story in one's mind, and, finally, the shrill, fussy voice of the ayah waking one for tea.

At school, we rested for a short time on low, folding cots on the veranda, and then we were expected to play games. During the hot part of the afternoon we played indoors, and after the shadows had begun to lengthen and the slight breeze of the evening had come up we moved outside to the wide courtyard.

I had never really grasped the system of competitive games. At home, whenever we played tag or guessing games, I was always allowed to "win"—"because," Mother used to tell Premila, "she is the youngest, and we have to allow for that." I had often heard her say it, and it seemed quite reasonable to me, but the result was that I had no clear idea of what "winning" meant.

When we played twos-and-threes that afternoon at school, in accordance with my training, I let one of the small English boys catch me, but was naturally rather puzzled when the other children did not return the courtesy. I ran about for what seemed like hours without ever catching anyone, until it was time for school to close. Much later I learned that my attitude was called "not being a good sport," and I stopped allowing myself to be caught, but it was not for years that I really learned the spirit of the thing.

When I saw our car come up to the school gate, I broke away from my classmates and rushed toward it yelling, "Ayah! Ayah!" It seemed like an eternity since I had seen her that morning—a wizened, affectionate figure in her white cotton sari, giving me dozens of urgent and useless instructions on how to be a good girl at school. Premila followed more sedately, and she told me on the way home never to do that again in front of the other children.

When we got home we went straight to Mother's high, white   23
room to have tea with her, and I immediately climbed onto the bed
and bounced gently up and down on the springs. Mother asked how
we had liked our first day in school. I was so pleased to be home and
to have left that peculiar Cynthia behind that I had nothing whatever
to say about school, except to ask what "apple" meant. But Premila
told Mother about the classes, and added that in her class they had
weekly tests to see if they had learned their lessons well.

I asked, "What's a test?"   24

Premila said, "You're too small to have them. You won't have   25
them in your class for donkey's years." She had learned the expression that day and was using it for the first time. We all laughed enormously at her wit. She also told Mother, in an aside, that we should
take sandwiches to school the next day. Not, she said, that *she*
minded. But they would be simpler for me to handle.

That whole lovely evening I didn't think about school at all. I   26
sprinted barefoot across the lawns with my favorite playmate, the
cook's son, to the stream at the end of the garden. We quarreled in our
usual way, waded in the tepid water under the lime trees, and waited
for the night to bring out the smell of the jasmine. I listened with fas-
cination to his stories of ghosts and demons, until I was too frightened
to cross the garden alone in the semidarkness. The ayah found me,
shouted at the cook's son, scolded me, hurried me in to supper—it
was an entirely usual, wonderful evening.

It was a week later, the day of Premila's first test, that our lives   27
changed rather abruptly. I was sitting at the back of my class, in my
usual inattentive way, only half listening to the teacher. I had started a
rather guarded friendship with the girl with the braids, whose name
turned out to be Nalini (Nancy, in school). The three other Indian
children were already fast friends. Even at that age it was apparent to
all of us that friendship with the English or Anglo-Indian children was
out of the question. Occasionally, during the class, my new friend and
I would draw pictures and show them to each other secretly.

The door opened sharply and Premila marched in. At first, the   28
teacher smiled at her in a kindly and encouraging way and said,
"Now, you're little Cynthia's sister?"

Premila didn't even look at her. She stood with her feet planted   29
firmly apart and her shoulders rigid, and addressed herself directly to
me. "Get up," she said. "We're going home."

I didn't know what had happened, but I was aware that it was a   30
crisis of some sort. I rose obediently and started to walk toward my
sister.

"Bring your pencils and your notebook," she said.   31

I went back for them, and together we left the room. The teacher   32
started to say something just as Premila closed the door, but we didn't
wait to hear what it was.

In complete silence we left the school grounds and started to walk   33
home. Then I asked Premila what the matter was. All she would say
was "We're going home for good."

It was a very tiring walk for a child of five and a half, and I   34
dragged along behind Premila with my pencils growing sticky in my
hand. I can still remember looking at the dusty hedges, and the tan-
gles of thorns in the ditches by the side of the road, smelling the faint
fragrance from the eucalyptus trees and wondering whether we would
ever reach home. Occasionally a horse-drawn tonga passed us, and
the women, in their pink or green silks, stared at Premila and me
trudging along on the side of the road. A few coolies and a line of
women carrying baskets of vegetables on their heads smiled at us.
But it was nearing the hottest time of day, and the road was almost
deserted. I walked more and more slowly, and shouted to Premila,
from time to time, "Wait for me!" with increasing peevishness. She
spoke to me only once, and that was to tell me to carry my notebook
on my head, because of the sun.

When we got to our house the ayah was just taking a tray of lunch   35
into Mother's room. She immediately started a long, worried questioning about what are you children doing back here at this hour of
the day.

Mother looked very startled and very concerned, and asked what   36
had happened.

Premila said, "We had our test today, and she made me and the   37
other Indians sit at the back of the room, with a desk between each
one."

Mother said, "Why was that, darling?"   38

"She said it was because Indians cheat," Premila added. "So I   39 don't think we should go back to that school."

Mother looked very distant, and was silent a long time. At last she   40 said, "Of course not, darling." She sounded displeased.

We all shared the curry she was having for lunch, and afterward I   41 was sent off to the beautifully familiar bedroom for my siesta. I could hear Mother and Premila talking through the open door.

Mother said, "Do you suppose she understood all that?"   42

Premila said, "I shouldn't think so. She's a baby."   43

Mother said, "Well, I hope it won't bother her."   44

Of course, they were both wrong. I understood it perfectly, and I   45 remember it all very clearly. But I put it happily away, because it had all happened to a girl called Cynthia, and I never was really particularly interested in her.

Focusing on the Story

1. What nationality are the two sisters? What nationality are the headmistress and the teachers at the Anglo-Indian school?
2. How did Santha feel about and react to her new name, Cynthia? Why couldn't the teachers remember Indian names? Had the headmistress just recently arrived in the country?
3. What was the economic status of Santha's family? Did they speak English? Give evidence from the story to support your answers.
4. Why did the Indian children have to sit in the back of the classroom? Why was friendship between the Indian and English children "out of the question"?
5. Why did the sisters abruptly leave school after one week? Were they coming back? What did Premila's teacher accuse Indian children of?

Interpreting and Evaluating

1. How were degrees from Indian schools regarded at that time? What may have been some reasons for this lack of recognition?

2. On the first day of school, Santha, or Cynthia, was bored and didn't seem to pay much attention. Was she a slow learner? Why did she find the word *apple* incomprehensible?
3. Why did Premila, or Pamela, want to take English sandwiches rather than Indian food to school? And why did Santha, or Cynthia, want to wear a dress rather than Indian clothes?
4. When Premila came to take Santha home on their last day at the English school, "she stood with her feet planted firmly apart and shoulders rigid." What can you infer about Premila's feelings from this description?
5. How did the English teachers stereotype the Indians? How did Santha and Premila react to this stereotyping? How may this stereo-typing have affected the Indian children's self-esteem in general?

Ideas for Writing and Further Discussion

1. Santha's short time at the British school in India obviously had a profound effect on her and probably changed her way of thinking for life. Write about a similar experience that has had a profound effect on your way of thinking. Describe what happened, and explain how and why it affected you so deeply.
   It's not necessary to write a formal thesis statement in a narrative essay, but you may wish to start with a general statement that expresses an attitude toward the experience.
2. What are some ways to overcome prejudice? Write an essay in which you explore two or three ways to deal with prejudice. Write an introduction that catches the reader's attention.
   Suggested *thesis*: two or three ways to deal with prejudice.
   Each *body paragraph* should include one specific way to overcome prejudice. Supply several reasons why each suggestion is a good way to deal with prejudice.

Mary

❖

Maya Angelou

About the Author

Maya Angelou, whose real name is Marguerite, was born in Arkansas in 1928. She spent much of her childhood with her grandmother and her brother, Bailey, in Stamps, Arkansas. At the age of eight, while staying with her mother in St. Louis, she was raped by her mother's boyfriend, Mr. Freeman, referred to in this story. For several years afterward, she refused to speak to anyone but her brother. A poet, Maya Angelou will long be remembered for the moving reading of her own poem at President Bill Clinton's inauguration.

Something to Think About

How do you react when someone insults you or talks down to you? Do you talk back? What if he or she is your boss?

Words to Keep in Mind

ecru *(1)* light tan color

tatting *(1)* making fine lace by looping and knotting cotton or linen thread with a special tatting shuttle

sacheted *(2)* perfumed with small bags of ground flower petals

impish *(3)* like a mischievous child

Cheshire cat *(12)* the grinning cat in *Alice in Wonderland*

Cupid *(12)* Roman god of love, often pictured as a small boy with a bow and arrows

barrenness *(13)* lack of ability to bear children

speckled *(14)* marked with spots

four-o'clocks *(22)* small trumpet-shaped red or white flowers that open in the late afternoon

dilemma *(37)* difficult choice

biddies *(37)* talkative women

Negro girls in small Southern towns, whether poverty-stricken or   1
just munching along on a few of life's necessities, were given as extensive and irrelevant preparations for adulthood as rich white girls shown in magazines. Admittedly the training was not the same. While white girls learned to waltz and sit gracefully with a tea cup balanced on their knees, we were lagging behind, learning the mid-Victorian values with very little money to indulge them. (Come and see Edna Lomax spending the money she made picking cotton on five balls of ecru tatting thread. Her fingers are bound to snag the work and she'll have to repeat the stitches time and time again. But she knows that when she buys the thread.)

We were required to embroider and I had trunkfuls of colorful   2
dishtowels, pillowcases, runners, and handkerchiefs to my credit. I mastered the art of crocheting and tatting, and there was a lifetime's supply of dainty doilies that would never be used in sacheted dresser drawers. It went without saying that all girls could iron and wash, but the finer touches around the home, like setting a table with real silver, baking roasts, and cooking vegetables without meat, had to be learned elsewhere. Usually at the source of those habits. During my tenth year, a white woman's kitchen became my finishing school.

Mrs. Viola Cullinan was a plump woman who lived in a three-   3
bedroom house somewhere behind the post office. She was singularly unattractive until she smiled, and then the lines around her eyes and mouth which made her look perpetually dirty disappeared, and her face looked like the mask of an impish elf. She usually rested her

smile until late afternoon when her women friends dropped in and Miss Glory, the cook, served them cold drinks on the closed-in porch.

The exactness of her house was inhuman. This glass went here 4 and only here. That cup had its place and it was an act of impudent rebellion to place it anywhere else. At twelve o'clock the table was set. At 12:15 Mrs. Cullinan sat down to dinner (whether her husband had arrived or not). At 12:16 Miss Glory brought out the food.

It took me a week to learn the difference between a salad plate, a 5 bread plate, and a dessert plate.

Mrs. Cullinan kept up the tradition of her wealthy parents. She 6 was from Virginia. Miss Glory, who was a descendant of slaves that had worked for the Cullinans, told me her history. She had married beneath her (according to Miss Glory). Her husband's family hadn't had their money very long and what they had "didn't 'mount to much."

As ugly as she was, I thought privately, she was lucky to get a 7 husband above or beneath her station. But Miss Glory wouldn't let me say a thing against her mistress. She was very patient with me, however, over the housework. She explained the dishware, silver-ware, and servants' bells.

The large round bowl in which soup was served wasn't a soup 8 bowl, it was a tureen. There were goblets, sherbet glasses, ice-cream glasses, wine glasses, green glass coffee cups with matching saucers, and water glasses. I had a glass to drink from, and it sat with Miss Glory's on a separate shelf from the others. Soup spoons, gravy boat, butter knives, salad forks, and carving platter were additions to my vocabulary and in fact almost represented a new language. I was fascinated with the novelty, with the fluttering Mrs. Cullinan and her Alice-in-Wonderland house.

Her husband remains, in my memory, undefined. I lumped him 9 with all the other white men that I had ever seen and tried not to see.

On our way home one evening, Miss Glory told me that Mrs. 10 Cullinan couldn't have children. She said that she was too delicate-boned. It was hard to imagine bones at all under those layers of fat. Miss Glory went on to say that the doctor had taken out all her lady organs. I reasoned that a pig's organs included the lungs, heart, and liver, so if Mrs. Cullinan was walking around without those essentials, it explained why she drank alcohol out of unmarked bottles. She was keeping herself embalmed.

When I spoke to Bailey about it, he agreed that I was right, but he 11 also informed me that Mr. Cullinan had two daughters by a colored lady and that I knew them very well. He added that the girls were the spitting image of their father. I was unable to remember what he looked like, although I had just left him a few hours before, but I thought of the Coleman girls. They were very light-skinned and certainly didn't look very much like their mother (no one ever mentioned Mr. Coleman).

My pity for Mrs. Cullinan preceded me the next morning like the 12 Cheshire cat's smile. Those girls, who could have been her daughters, were beautiful. They didn't have to straighten their hair. Even when they were caught in the rain, their braids still hung down straight like tamed snakes. Their mouths were pouty little Cupid's bows. Mrs. Cullinan didn't know what she missed. Or maybe she did. Poor Mrs. Cullinan.

For weeks after, I arrived early, left late, and tried very hard to 13 make up for her barrenness. If she had had her own children, she wouldn't have had to ask me to run a thousand errands from her back door to the back door of her friends. Poor old Mrs. Cullinan.

Then one evening Miss Glory told me to serve the ladies on the 14 porch. After I set the tray down and turned toward the kitchen, one of the women asked, "What's your name, girl?" It was the speckled-faced one. Mrs. Cullinan said, "She doesn't talk much. Her name's Margaret."

"Is she dumb?" 15

"No. As I understand it, she can talk when she wants to but she's 16 usually quiet as a little mouse. Aren't you, Margaret?"

I smiled at her. Poor thing. No organs and couldn't even pronounce my name correctly. 17

"She's a sweet little thing, though." 18

"Well, that may be, but the name's too long. I'd never bother 19 myself. I'd call her Mary if I was you."

I fumed into the kitchen. That horrible woman would never have 20 the chance to call me Mary because if I was starving I'd never work for her. I decided I wouldn't pee on her if her heart was on fire. Giggles drifted in off the porch and into Miss Glory's pots. I wondered what they could be laughing about.

Whitefolks were so strange. Could they be talking about me?   21 Everybody knew that they stuck together better than the Negroes did. It was possible that Mrs. Cullinan had friends in St. Louis who heard about a girl from Stamps being in court and wrote to tell her. Maybe she knew about Mr. Freeman.

My lunch was in my mouth a second time and I went outside and   22 relieved myself on the bed of four-o'clocks. Miss Glory thought I might be coming down with something and told me to go on home, that Momma would give me some herb tea, and she'd explain to her mistress.

I realized how foolish I was being before I reached the pond. Of   23 course Mrs. Cullinan didn't know. Otherwise she wouldn't have given me the two nice dresses that Momma cut down, and she certainly wouldn't have called me a "sweet little thing." My stomach felt fine, and I didn't mention anything to Momma.

That evening I decided to write a poem on being white, fat, old,   24 and without children. It was going to be a tragic ballad. I would have to watch her carefully to capture the essence of her loneliness and pain.

The very next day, she called me by the wrong name. Miss Glory   25 and I were washing up the lunch dishes when Mrs. Cullinan came to the doorway. "Mary?"

Miss Glory asked, "Who?"   26

Mrs. Cullinan, sagging a little, knew and I knew. "I want Mary to   27 go down to Mrs. Randall's and take her some soup. She's not been feeling well for a few days."

Miss Glory's face was a wonder to see. "You mean Margaret,   28 ma'am. Her name's Margaret."

"That's too long. She's Mary from now on. Heat that soup from   29 last night and put it in the china tureen and, Mary, I want you to carry it carefully."

Every person I knew had a hellish horror of being "called out of   30 his own name." It was a dangerous practice to call a Negro anything that could be loosely construed as insulting because of the centuries of their having been called niggers, jigs, dinges, blackbirds, crows, boots, and spooks.

Miss Glory had a fleeting second of feeling sorry for me. Then as she handed me the hot tureen she said, "Don't mind, don't pay that no mind. Sticks and stones may break your bones, but words . . . You know, I been working for her for twenty years." 31

She held the back door open for me. "Twenty years. I wasn't much older than you. My name used to be Hallelujah. That's what Ma named me, but my mistress give me 'Glory,' and it stuck. I likes it better too." 32

I was in the little path that ran behind the houses when Miss Glory shouted, "It's shorter too." 33

For a few seconds it was a toss up over whether I would laugh (imagine being named Hallelujah) or cry (imagine letting some white woman rename you for her convenience). My anger saved me from either outburst. I had to quit the job, but the problem was going to be how to do it. Momma wouldn't allow me to quit for just any reason. 34

"She's a peach. That woman is a real peach." Mrs. Randall's maid was talking as she took the soup from me, and I wondered what her name used to be and what she answered to now. 35

For a week I looked into Mrs. Cullinan's face as she called me Mary. She ignored my coming late and leaving early. Miss Glory was a little annoyed because I had begun to leave egg yolk on the dishes and wasn't putting much heart in polishing the silver. I hoped that she would complain to our boss, but she didn't. 36

Then Bailey solved my dilemma. He had me describe the contents of the cupboard and the particular plates she liked best. Her favorite piece was a casserole shaped like a fish and the green glass coffee cups. I kept his instructions in mind, so on the next day when Miss Glory was hanging out clothes and I had again been told to serve the old biddies on the porch, I dropped the empty serving tray. When I heard Mrs. Cullinan scream, "Mary!" I picked up the casserole and two of the green glass cups in readiness. As she rounded the kitchen door I let them fall on the tiled floor. 37

I could never absolutely describe to Bailey what happened next, because each time I got to the part where she fell on the floor and screwed up her ugly face to cry, we burst out laughing. She actually 38 wobbled around on the floor and picked up shards of the cups and cried, "Oh, Momma. Oh, dear Gawd. It's Momma's china from Virginia. Oh, Momma, I sorry."

Miss Glory came running in from the yard and the women from   39
the porch crowded around. Miss Glory was almost as broken up as her mistress. "You mean to say she broke our Virginia dishes? What we gone do?"

Mrs. Cullinan cried louder, "That clumsy nigger. Clumsy little   40
black nigger."

Old speckled-face leaned down and asked, "Who did it, Viola?   41
Was it Mary? Who did it?"

Everything was happening so fast I can't remember whether her   42
action preceded her words, but I know that Mrs. Cullinan said, "Her name's Margaret, goddamn it, her name's Margaret!" And she threw a wedge of the broken plate at me. It could have been the hysteria which put her aim off, but the flying crockery caught Miss Glory right over her ear and she started screaming.

I left the front door wide open so all the neighbors could hear.   43

Mrs. Cullinan was right about one thing. My name wasn't Mary.   44

Focusing on the Story

1. List some tasks that African-American girls had to learn in preparation for adulthood in the 1930s and 1940s, the time the story takes place. How were they similar to the tasks that white girls had to master? How were they different?
2. Describe Mrs. Viola Cullinan, the white woman in whose service Margaret, or Marguerite, learned "the finer touches around the home." How did Margaret feel about working in the house at first?
3. In paragraph 4, the author writes that "the exactness of [Mrs. Viola Cullinan's] house was inhuman." What does this mean?
4. What was Miss Glory's real name? Why did Mrs. Cullinan change it? Why did she suddenly start to call Margaret "Mary"? How did Margaret feel about working for Mrs. Cullinan after being called "Mary"?
5. What did Margaret hope to achieve by breaking the casserole and the green glass coffee cups?

Interpreting and Evaluating

1. In paragraph 1, the author writes that "girls in small Southern towns . . . were given . . . irrelevant preparations for adulthood." Such preparations are in fact common in many cultures. Why may such customs be maintained? How may traditions be both a hindrance to progress and something to be cherished?
2. While staying with her mother in St. Louis, Maya Angelou was raped by her mother's boyfriend, Mr. Freeman. In paragraphs 21, 22, and 23, her thoughts focus on that incident. How does she feel about it? Why did she feel that if Mrs. Cullinan had known about it, she wouldn't have given her "the nice dresses" nor called her a "sweet little thing"?
3. Why is the author, who today is known by the name "Maya," so upset about being called "Mary" rather than Margaret? After all, calling people by their shorter nicknames is a common practice in the United States. What is different in this situation? How would you have handled it if you had been in Margaret's place?
4. How would you characterize Margaret? How is she different from Miss Glory? Use examples from the story to illustrate your point.
5. The tone of a story reflects the author's attitude to the subject matter. How would you describe the tone of this story? Point out specific words and phrases the author has chosen to convey this tone.

Ideas for Writing and Further Discussion

1. Do you remember your first job? Write two or three paragraphs describing your first job. How old were you? What was your employer like? What did you have to do? How much money did you make? How did it make you feel?
2. Does your family maintain a unique tradition? Write a paragraph or two describing a special tradition in your family. How do you feel about it?
3. Mrs. Viola Cullinan is driven by her daily routine: lunch is served at 12:16 every day; her lady friends drop in every afternoon. Write

three or four paragraphs describing the routine in your own household.

It's not necessary to write a formal thesis statement in a narrative essay, but you may wish to start with a general statement that expresses an attitude toward the experience.

Victims

of

Armed

Conflict

Just Lather, That's All

❖

Hernando Téllez

About the Author

Hernando Téllez, born in 1908, is a Colombian politician, diplomat, and author who often writes about political conflicts in South America.

 ### Something to Think About

How does murdering someone with a knife or a razor at close range differ from executing or killing someone in an armed conflict? Which form of killing might be more difficult?

Words to Keep in Mind

lather *(title)* foam formed by soap

strop *(1)* thick leather strap used to sharpen razors

fatigue *(9)* exhaustion, tiredness

caress *(9)* gentle touch

feigned *(9)* pretended

faction *(9)* a group working for a common cause against, for example, the government

imposes *(9)* places, sets forth, often by authority or force

emitted *(9)* let out

conscientious *(9)* doing what one knows is right; honest

swirls *(10)* curls

rejuvenated *(11)* made young

ineradicable *(11)* cannot be gotten rid of or removed

avenger *(11)* one who wants to punish justly for something wrong

He said nothing when he entered. I was passing the best of my 1
razors back and forth on a strop. When I recognized him I started to
tremble. But he didn't notice. Hoping to conceal my emotion, I continued sharpening the razor. I tested it on the meat of my thumb, and
then held it up to the light. At that moment he took off the bullet-
studded belt that his gun holster dangled from. He hung it up on a
wall hook and placed his military cap over it. Then he turned to me,
loosening the knot of his tie, and said, "It's hot as hell. Give me a
shave." He sat in the chair.

I estimated he had a four-day beard. The four days taken up by the 2
latest expedition in search of our troops. His face seemed reddened,
burned by the sun. Carefully, I began to prepare the soap. I cut off a
few slices, dropped them into the cup, mixed in a bit of warm water,
and began to stir with the brush. Immediately the foam began to rise.
"The other boys in the group should have this much beard, too." I
continued stirring the lather.

"But we did all right, you know. We got the main ones. We 3
brought back some dead, and we've got some others still alive. But
pretty soon they'll all be dead."

"How many did you catch?" I asked. 4

"Fourteen. We had to go pretty deep into the woods to find them. 5
But we'll get even. Not one of them comes out of this alive, not one."
He leaned back on the chair when he saw me with the lather-covered
brush in my hand. I still had to put the sheet on him. No doubt about
it, I was upset. I took a sheet out of a drawer and knotted it around my

---

"Just Lather, That's All" from *Ashes from the Wind and Other Tales* by Hernando
Téllez. © 1950 by Hernando Téllez. Reprinted with the permission of *Américas,* a
bimonthly magazine published by the General Secretariat of the Organization of
American States in English and Spanish.

customer's neck. He wouldn't stop talking. He probably thought I was in sympathy with his party.

"The town must have learned a lesson from what we did the other 6 day," he said.

"Yes," I replied, securing the knot at his dark, sweaty neck. 7

"That was a fine show, eh?" 8

"Very good," I answered, turning back for the brush. The man 9 closed his eyes with a gesture of fatigue and sat waiting for the cool caress of the soap. I had never had him so close to me. The day he ordered the whole town to file into the patio of the school to see the four rebels hanging there, I came face-to-face with him for an instant. But the sight of the mutilated bodies kept me from noticing the face of the man who had directed it all, the face I was now about to take into my hands. It was not an unpleasant face, certainly. And the beard, which made him seem a bit older than he was, didn't suit him badly at all. His name was Torres. Captain Torres. A man of imagination, because who else would have thought of hanging the naked rebels and then holding target practice on certain parts of their bodies? I began to apply the first layer of soap. With his eyes closed, he continued. "Without any effort I could go straight to sleep," he said, "but there's plenty to do this afternoon." I stopped the lathering and asked with a feigned lack of interest: "A firing squad?" "Something like that, but a little slower." I got on with the job of lathering his beard. My hands started trembling again. The man could not possibly realize it, and this was in my favor. But I would have preferred that he hadn't come. It was likely that many of our faction had seen him enter. And an enemy under one's roof imposes certain conditions. I would be obliged to shave that beard like any other one, carefully, gently, like that of any customer, taking pains to see that no single pore emitted a drop of blood. Being careful to see that the little tufts of hair did not lead the blade astray. Seeing that his skin ended up clean, soft, and healthy, so that passing the back of my hand over it I couldn't feel a hair. Yes, I was secretly a rebel, but I was also a conscientious barber, and proud of the preciseness of my profession. And this four days' growth of beard was a fitting challenge.

I took the razor, opened up the two protective arms, exposed the 10 blade and began the job, from one of the sideburns downward. The razor responded beautifully. His beard was inflexible and hard, not too long, but thick. Bit by bit the skin emerged. The razor rasped along, making its customary sound as fluffs of lather mixed with bits of hair gathered along the blade. I paused a moment to clean it, then took up the strop again to sharpen the razor, because I'm a barber who does things properly. The man, who had kept his eyes closed, opened them now, removed one of his hands from under the sheet, felt the spot on his face where the soap had been cleared off, and said, "Come to the school today at six o'clock." "The same thing as the other day?" I asked, horrified. "It could be better," he replied. "What do you plan to do?" "I don't know yet. But we'll amuse ourselves." Once more he leaned back and closed his eyes. I approached him with the razor poised. "Do you plan to punish them all?" I ventured timidly. "All." The soap was drying on his face. I had to hurry. In the mirror I looked toward the street. It was the same as ever: the grocery store with two or three customers in it. Then I glanced at the clock: two twenty in the afternoon. The razor continued on its downward stroke. Now from the other sideburn down. A thick, blue beard. He should have let it grow like some poets or priests do. It would suit him well. A lot of people wouldn't recognize him. Much to his benefit, I thought, as I attempted to cover the neck area smoothly. There, for sure, the razor had to be handled masterfully, since the hair, although softer, grew into little swirls. A curly beard. One of the tiny pores could be opened up and issue forth its pearl of blood. A good barber such as I prides himself on never allowing this to happen to a client. And this was a first-class client. How many of us had he ordered shot? How many of us had he ordered mutilated? It was better not to think about it. Torres did not know that I was his enemy. He did not know it nor did the rest. It was a secret shared by very few, precisely so that I could inform the revolutionaries of what Torres was doing in the town and of what he was planning each time he undertook a rebel-hunting excursion. So it was going to be very difficult to explain that I had him right in my hands and let him go peacefully—alive and shaved.

The beard was now almost completely gone. He seemed younger, less burdened by years than when he had arrived. I suppose this always happens with men who visit barbershops. Under the stroke of

11

my razor Torres was being rejuvenated—rejuvenated because I am a good barber, the best in the town, if I may say so. A little more lather here, under his chin, on his Adam's apple, on this big vein. How hot it is getting! Torres must be sweating as much as I. But he is not afraid. He is a calm man, who is not even thinking about what he is going to do with the prisoners this afternoon. On the other hand I, with this razor in my hands, stroking and restroking this skin, trying to keep blood from oozing from these pores, can't even think clearly. Damn him for coming, because I'm a revolutionary and not a murderer. And how easy it would be to kill him. And he deserves it. Does he? No! What the devil! No one deserves to have someone else make the sacrifice of becoming a murderer. What do you gain by it? Nothing. Others come along and still others, and the first ones kill the second ones and they the next ones and it goes on like this until everything is a sea of blood. I could cut this throat just so, zip! zip! I wouldn't give him time to complain and since he has his eyes closed he wouldn't see the glistening knife blade or my glistening eyes. But I'm trembling like a real murderer. Out of his neck a gush of blood would spout onto the sheet, on the chair, on my hands, on the floor. I would have to close the door. And the blood would keep inching along the floor, warm, ineradicable, uncontainable, until it reached the street, like a little scarlet stream. I'm sure that one solid stroke, one deep incision, would prevent any pain. He wouldn't suffer. But what would I do with the body? Where would I hide it? I would have to flee, leaving all I have behind, and take refuge far away, far, far away. But they would follow until they found me. "Captain Torres' murderer. He slit his throat while he was shaving him—a coward." And then on the other side. "The avenger of us all. A name to remember. (And here they would mention my name.) He was the town barber. No one knew he was defending our cause."

And what of all this? Murderer or hero? My destiny depends on 12 the edge of this blade. I can turn my hand a bit more, press a little harder on the razor, and sink it in. The skin would give way like silk, like rubber, like the strop. There is nothing more tender than human skin and the blood is always there, ready to pour forth. A blade like this doesn't fail. It is my best. But I don't want to be a murderer, no sir. You came to me for a shave. And I perform my work honorably. . . . I

don't want blood on my hands. Just lather, that's all. You are an execu-
tioner and I am only a barber. Each person has his own place in the
scheme of things. That's right. His own place.

Now his chin had been stroked clean and smooth. The man sat up   13
and looked into the mirror. He rubbed his hands over his skin and felt
it fresh, like new.

"Thanks," he said. He went to the hanger for his belt, pistol and   14
cap. I must have been very pale; my shirt felt soaked. Torres finished
adjusting the buckle, straightened his pistol in the holster and after
automatically smoothing down his hair, he put on the cap. From his
pants pocket he took out several coins to pay me for my services. And
he began to head toward the door. In the doorway he paused for a
moment, and turning to me he said:

"They told me that you'd kill me. I came to find out. But killing   15
isn't easy. You can take my word for it." And he headed on down the
street.

Focusing on the Story

1. Who is Captain Torres, the barber's customer? Who or what does he
   represent? With which side does the barber sympathize?
2. Where has Captain Torres been for the last four days? What has he
   been up to during this time?
3. What does Captain Torres plan to do with the captured rebels who
   are still alive?
4. An internal conflict is a conflict within a character. What is the barber's internal conflict or dilemma?
5. Why does the barber decide not to kill Torres?

Interpreting and Evaluating

1. The setting (time and place) of the story is a barber shop on a hot
   day. However, the reader must infer in what country the action
   occurs. On what continent is the country? What is happening politi-
   cally in this country?
2. The barber says that his ties to the revolution were kept secret so
   that he could inform the revolutionaries of what Torres was up to.
   Why would the barber be a good choice for an informer?

3. If the barber had killed Torres, how might the barber have been considered a cowardly murderer on one hand and a heroic avenger on the other?

4. At the end of the story the reader learns that Captain Torres has been told that the barber would kill him, yet Torres remains completely cool while the barber is trembling and sweating. Is Torres a fool to let the barber get so close to him with a sharp razor? What does Torres know about human behavior?

5. Should the barber be praised or criticized for his action? Should he have killed Captain Torres, who, after all, had killed several of the barber's comrades? Explain.

An Idea for Writing and Further Discussion

Have you ever been faced with a difficult decision? What was your dilemma? What did you finally decide to do? Write about a time when you were faced with a difficult decision. Describe your dilemma, and explain why you finally chose to make the decision that you made.

It's not necessary to write a formal thesis statement in a narrative essay, but you may wish to start with a general statement that expresses an attitude toward the experience.

Old Man at
the Bridge

❖

Ernest Hemingway

About the Author

Ernest Hemingway was born in Indiana in 1899. During World War I, he served as an ambulance driver on the Italian front, and after the war had ended he returned to Europe as a foreign correspondent. In 1954, Hemingway received the Nobel Prize for literature but died only seven years later by suicide.

Something to Think About

Are violence and war inevitable? Who suffers the most in war? What is the best way for men and women to face physical danger?

Words to Keep in Mind

spectacles *(1)* eyeglasses

pontoons *(1)* cylinders filled with air to support a temporary bridge

Ebro Delta *(11)* area where the Ebro river flows into the Mediterranean near Barcelona

Fascists *(36)* Spanish troops under General Franco in the Spanish Civil War in 1936

An old man with steel rimmed spectacles and very dusty clothes   1
sat by the side of the road. There was a pontoon bridge across the
river and carts, trucks, and men, women and children were crossing it.
The mule-drawn carts staggered up the steep bank from the bridge
with soldiers helping push against the spokes of the wheels. The
trucks ground up and away heading out of it all and the peasants plod-
ded along in the ankle deep dust. But the old man sat there without
moving. He was too tired to go any farther.

It was my business to cross the bridge, explore the bridgehead   2
beyond and find out to what point the enemy had advanced. I did this
and returned over the bridge. There were not so many carts now and
very few people on foot, but the old man was still there.

"Where do you come from?" I asked him.   3

"From San Carlos," he said, and smiled.   4

That was his native town and so it gave him pleasure to mention it   5
and he smiled.

"I was taking care of animals," he explained.   6

"Oh," I said, not quite understanding.   7

"Yes," he said, "I stayed, you see, taking care of animals. I was   8
the last one to leave the town of San Carlos."

He did not look like a shepherd nor a herdsman and I looked at his   9
black dusty clothes and his gray dusty face and his steel rimmed spectacles and said, "What animals were they?"

"Various animals," he said, and shook his head. "I had to leave   10
them."

I was watching the bridge and the African looking country of the   11
Ebro Delta and wondering how long now it would be before we
would see the enemy, and listening all the while for the first noises
that would signal that ever mysterious event called contact, and the
old man still sat there.

"What animals were they?" I asked.   12

"There were three animals altogether," he explained. "There were   13
two goats and a cat and then there were four pairs of pigeons."

"And you had to leave them?" I asked.   14

"Yes. Because of the artillery. The captain told me to go because   15
of the artillery."

"And you have no family?" I asked, watching the far end of the   16
bridge where a few last carts were hurrying down the slope of the
bank.

"No" he said, "only the animals I stated. The cat, of course, will   17
be all right. A cat can look out for itself, but I cannot think what will
become of the others."

"What politics have you?" I asked.   18

"I am without politics," he said. "I am seventy-six years old. I   19
have come twelve kilometers now and I think now I can go no further."

"This is not a good place to stop," I said. "If you can make it,   20
there are trucks up the road where it forks for Tortosa."

"I will wait a while," he said, "and then I will go. Where do the   21
trucks go?"

"Towards Barcelona," I told him.   22

"I know no one in that direction," he said, "but thank you very   23
much. Thank you again very much."

He looked at me very blankly and tiredly, then said, having to   24
share his worry with someone, "The cat will be all right, I am sure.
There is no need to be unquiet about the cat. But the others. Now
what do you think about the others?"

"Why they'll probably come through it all right."   25

"You think so?"   26

"Why not," I said, watching the far bank where now there were   27
no carts.

"But what will they do under the artillery when I was told to leave   28
because of the artillery?"

"Did you leave the dove cage unlocked?" I asked.   29

"Yes."   30

"Then they'll fly."   31

"Yes, certainly they'll fly. But the others. It's better not to think   32
about the others," he said.

"If you are rested I would go," I urged. "Get up and try to walk   33
now."

"Thank you," he said and got to his feet, swayed from side to side   34
and then sat down backwards in the dust.

"I was taking care of animals," he said dully, but no longer to me.   35
"I was only taking care of animals."

There was nothing to do about him. It was Easter Sunday and the   36
Fascists were advancing toward the Ebro. It was a gray overcast day
with a low ceiling so their planes were not up. That and the fact that
cats know how to look after themselves was all the good luck that old
man would ever have.

Focusing on the Story

1. Why are carts, trucks, men, women, and children crossing the
   bridge? What's going on?
2. The setting (place and time) of the story is not stated directly but
   rather implied. In what country and during which time does the
   story take place?
3. Who is the narrator (the character who tells the story), and what can
   you say about him? What is his job?
4. Describe the old man. What animals has the old man left behind?
   Which ones is he most worried about? What's the irony in this situation?
5. How is the old man lucky on the particular day the narrator meets
   him?

Interpreting and Evaluating

1. Why does the old man smile when he tells the narrator that he is
   from San Carlos? Why doesn't he want to go to Barcelona? Doesn't
   he realize the danger he is in?
2. The narrator asks the old man what politics he has. What does this
   question mean? Would the outcome have changed for the old man if
   his answer had been different?
3. A symbol is something that has meaning beyond the most obvious
   literal meaning. For example, a flag is just a piece of cloth but often

symbolizes a country or state. What do doves usually symbolize? How may the bridge in this story be considered a symbol, and what may the bridge symbolize?

4. The old man keeps repeating that he was only taking care of his animals. Nevertheless, what will most likely happen to him the next day or in the next few days? Do you feel sorry for the old man? How does the old man face the situation? If you had been in the old man's place, would you have shown more signs of fear?

5. What was Hemingway's opinion of war, judging from this story?

Ideas for Writing and Further Discussion

1. Write a paragraph or two about a time when you tried to help someone but couldn't. Describe the situation, and explain why the other person refused your help. How did the incident make you feel?

2. Have you ever had to face a dangerous situation head on? How did you feel and how did you react? Write a narrative essay about a dangerous or frightening experience you have had. Describe what happened and how you handled it. How did you feel? What was the outcome? Did you learn anything about your own feelings from the experience?

   It's not necessary to write a formal thesis statement in a narrative essay, but you may wish to start with a general statement that expresses your attitude toward the experience.

3. Think of the message or theme that Hemingway's story "Old Man at the Bridge" conveys to the reader. Do innocent people suffer in wars? How does Hemingway convey the message that innocent people suffer in wars?

   Write an essay in which you discuss the different techniques that Hemingway uses to convey the reality of war. For example, when he describes the old man, he selects only details that make us feel sorry for the man: he's old, alone, tired, and confused. How does the old man feel about the animals? How does the soldier feel about the old man and the situation in general? Do the symbols contribute to the theme?

   Suggested *thesis:* two or three ways that the author tries to convey the message that innocent people suffer in wars. Each *body paragraph* should explore one such way.

Humor
and
Satire

Fresh Air Will Kill You

❖

Art Buchwald

About the Author

Art Buchwald was born in 1925 and grew up in foster homes in New York during the Great Depression. He worked since he was nine years old, dropped out of school and joined the Navy when he was 17. A two-time Pulitzer Prize winner, he is famous worldwide for his column of political satire and humor which appears in over 530 newspapers.

Something to Think About

Are grim issues such as pollution a laughing matter? How can humor help us to focus on serious questions?

Words to Keep in Mind

smog *(1)* harmful mixture of fog and smoke
odor *(6)* smell

Smog, which was once the big attraction of Los Angeles, can now   1
be found all over the country from Butte, Montana, to New York City,

and people are getting so used to polluted air that it's very difficult for them to breathe anything else.

I was lecturing recently, and one of my stops was Flagstaff, 2 Arizona, which is about seven thousand miles above sea level.

As soon as I got out of the plane, I smelled something peculiar.   3

"What's that smell?" I asked the man who met me at the plane.   4

"I don't smell anything," he replied.   5

"There's definitely an odor that I'm not familiar with," I said.   6

"Oh, you must be talking about the fresh air. A lot of people come 7 out here who have never smelled fresh air before."

"What's it supposed to do?" I asked suspiciously.   8

"Nothing. You just breathe it like any other kind of air. It's sup- 9 posed to be good for your lungs."

"I've heard that story before," I said.   10

"How come if it's air, my eyes aren't itching and watering?"   11

"Your eyes don't water with fresh air. That's the advantage of it. 12 Saves you a lot in paper tissues."

I looked around and everything appeared crystal clear. It was a 13 strange sensation and made me feel very uncomfortable.

My host, sensing this, tried to be reassuring. "Please don't worry 14 about it. Tests have proved that you can breathe fresh air day and night without its doing any harm to the body."

"You're just saying that because you don't want me to leave," I 15 said. "Nobody who has lived in a major city can stand fresh air for a very long time. He has no tolerance for it."

"Well, if the fresh air bothers you, why don't you put a handker- 16 chief over your nose and breathe through your mouth?"

"Okay, I'll try it. If I'd known I was coming to a place that had 17 nothing but fresh air, I would have brought a surgical mask to protect myself."

We drove in silence. About fifteen minutes later he asked, "How 18 do you feel now?"

"Okay, I guess, but I miss sneezing."   19

"We don't sneeze too much here," the man admitted. "Do they 20 sneeze a lot where you come from?"

"All the time. There are some days when that's all you do."   21

"Do you enjoy it?"   22

"Not necessarily, but if you don't sneeze, you'll die. Let me ask   23
you something. How come there's no air pollution around here?"

"Flagstaff can't seem to attract industry. I guess we're really   24
behind in the times. The only smoke we get is when the Indians start
signaling each other. But the wind seems to blow it away."

The fresh air was making me feel dizzy. "Isn't there a diesel bus   25
around here that I could breathe into for a couple of hours?"

"Not at this time of day. I might be able to find a truck for you."   26

We found a truck driver, and slipped him a five-dollar bill, and he   27
let me put my head near his exhaust pipe for a half hour. I was immediately revived and able to give my speech.

Nobody was as happy to leave Flagstaff as I was. My next stop   28
was Los Angeles, and when I got off the plane, I took one big deep
breath of the smog-filled air, my eyes started to water, I began to
sneeze, and I felt like a new man again.

Focusing on the Story

1. What was the odor in Flagstaff, Arizona, that seemed strange to
   Buchwald?
2. Why did the air in Flagstaff make Buchwald feel very uncomfortable, even dizzy?
3. According to Buchwald's host, when is the only time people see
   smoke in Flagstaff?
4. What did the author finally do to cure his dizziness?
5. How did Buchwald react when he arrived in Los Angeles?

Interpreting and Evaluating

1. What accounts for the humor in this essay?
2. What is Buchwald making fun of?
3. Although the essay is intended to be humorous, what important
   issue does Buchwald focus on?
4. How could ridiculing a serious issue be harmful?

Ideas for Writing and Further Discussion

1. Although essays of humor and satire are difficult to write, give it a try. Focus on a serious issue such as global warming or an important political question, and try to look at it from a humorous or mocking perspective. For example, Buchwald says that smog "was once the big *attraction* of Los Angeles." Calling something the opposite of what it is often leads to humor. Exaggeration may also lead to humor. For instance, Buchwald says that Flagstaff is "seven thousand miles above sea level" when it is in fact less than 7,000 feet above sea level. Ridiculous images such as sticking your head in an exhaust pipe to breathe diesel fumes furthermore bring about laughter.

2. Most of us like to travel in order to see and experience new and often strange places. Write an essay about a trip you took. Did you travel by car, plane, ship, or train? Who did you travel with? What was the purpose of your trip? How were the new places different from your home? Describe some of these differences. How did you feel after you returned home to your familiar surroundings?

Harrison Bergeron

❖

Kurt Vonnegut, Jr.

About the Author

Kurt Vonnegut, Jr., an American novelist and writer, was born in Indianapolis, Indiana, in 1922. In his writing, Vonnegut often ridicules firmly held beliefs and shows the dehumanizing effects they sometimes have.

Something to Think About

What would it be like to live in a society where no one is allowed to compete, where no one is better educated or better looking than anyone else? Is such a society really ideal? What will happen to our society if human intelligence and thought are no longer valued?

Words to Keep in Mind

vigilance (1) watch; surveillance

winced *(11)* shrank or drew back as if in pain

doozy *(22)* something bad

impediment *(37)* defect; obstacle

luminous *(41)* bright; clear

grackle *(42)* any American blackbird

squawk *(42)* loud, harsh cry

consternation *(49)* fear; panic

bellowed *(55)* called in a deep hollow voice (like a sound made by a cow)

hobbled *(55)* legs tied together with a short rope

harness *(56)* straps and bands put on a wearer to attach gear

flounced *(73)* moved impatiently or angrily

capered *(73)* leaped or skipped around

gamboled *(73)* danced around; frolicked

The year was 2081, and everybody was finally equal. They weren't 1
only equal before God and the law. They were equal every which
way. Nobody was smarter than anybody else. Nobody was better
looking than anybody else. Nobody was stronger or quicker than anybody else. All this equality was due to the 211th, 212th, and 213th
Amendments to the Constitution, and to the unceasing vigilance of
agents of the United States Handicapper General.

Some things about living still weren't quite right, though. April, 2
for instance, still drove people crazy by not being springtime. And it
was in that clammy month that the H-G men took George and Hazel
Bergeron's fourteen-year-old son, Harrison, away.

It was tragic, all right, but George and Hazel couldn't think about 3
it very hard. Hazel had a perfectly average intelligence, which meant
she couldn't think about anything except in short bursts. And George,
while his intelligence was way above normal, had a little mental
handicap radio in his ear. He was required by law to wear it at all
times. It was tuned to a government transmitter. Every twenty seconds or so, the transmitter would send out some sharp noise to keep
people like George from taking unfair advantage or their brains.

George and Hazel were watching television. There were tears on 4
Hazel's cheeks, but she'd forgotten for the moment what they were
about.

On the television screen were ballerinas.   5

A buzzer sounded in George's head. His thoughts fled in panic,   6
like bandits from a burglar alarm.

"That was a real pretty dance, that dance they just did," said   7
Hazel.

"Huh?" said George.   8

"That dance—it was nice," said Hazel.   9

"Yup," said George. He tried to think a little about the ballerinas.   10
They weren't really very good—no better than anybody else would
have been, anyway. They were burdened with sashweights and bags
of birdshot, and their faces were masked, so that no one, seeing a free
and graceful gesture or pretty face, would feel like something the cat
drug in. George was toying with the vague notion that maybe dancers
shouldn't be handicapped. But he didn't get very far with it before
another noise in his ear radio scattered his thoughts.

George winced. So did two of the eight ballerinas.   11

Hazel saw him wince. Having no mental handicap herself, she   12
had to ask George what the latest sound had been.

"Sounded like somebody hitting a milk bottle with a ball peen   13
hammer," said George.

"I'd think it would be real interesting, hearing all the different   14
sounds," said Hazel, a little envious. "All the things they think up."

"Um," said George.   15

"Only, if I was a Handicapper General, you know what I would   16
do?" said Hazel. Hazel, as a matter of fact, bore a strong resemblance
to the Handicapper General, a woman named Diana Moon Glampers.
"If I was Diana Moon Glampers," said Hazel, "I'd have chimes on
Sunday—just chimes. Kind of in honor or religion."

"I could think, if it was just chimes," said George.   17

"Well—maybe make 'em real loud," said Hazel. "I think I'd   18
make a good Handicapper General."

"Good as anybody else," said George.   19

"Who knows better'n I do what normal is?" Hazel said.   20

"Right," said George. He began to think glimmeringly about his   21
abnormal son who was now in jail, about Harrison, but a twenty-one
gun salute in his head stopped that.

"Boy!" said Hazel, "that was a doozy, wasn't it?"   22

It was such a doozy that George was white and trembling, and   23
tears stood on the rims of his red eyes. Two of the eight ballerinas had
collapsed to the studio floor and were holding their temples.

"All of a sudden you look so tired," said Hazel. "Why don't you   24
stretch out on the sofa, so's you can rest your handicap bag on the pil-
lows, honeybunch." She was referring to the forty-seven pounds of
birdshot in a canvas bag, which was padlocked around George's neck.
"Go on and rest the bag for a while," she said. "I don't care if you're
not equal to me for a while."

George weighed the bag with his hands. "I don't mind it," he said.   25
I don't notice it anymore. It's part of me."

"You've been so tired lately—kind of wore out," said Hazel. "If   26
there was just some way we could make a little hole in the bottom of
the bag and just take out a few of them lead balls. Just a few."

"Two years in prison and two thousand dollars fine for every ball   27
I took out," said George. "I don't call that a bargain."

"If you could just take out a few when you came home from   28
work," said Hazel. "I mean—you don't compete with anybody
around here. You just set around."

"If I tried to get away with it," said George, "then other people'd   29
get away with it—and pretty soon we'd be right back to the dark ages
again, with everybody competing against everybody else. You
wouldn't like that, would you?"

"I'd hate it," said Hazel.   30

"There you are," said George. "The minute people start cheating   31
on laws, what do you think happens to society?"

If Hazel hadn't been able to come up with an answer to this ques-   32
tion, George couldn't have supplied one. A siren was going off in his
head.

"Reckon it'd fall all apart," said Hazel.   33

"What would?" said George blankly.   34

"Society," said Hazel uncertainly. "Wasn't that what you just   35
said?"

"Who knows?" said George.   36

The television program was suddenly interrupted for a news bul-   37
letin. It wasn't clear at first as to what the bulletin was about, since
the announcer, like all announcers, had a serious speech impediment.

For about half a minute, and in a state of high excitement, the announcer tried to say, "Ladies and gentlemen—"

He finally gave up, handed the bulletin to a ballerina to read.   38

"That's all right—" Hazel said of the announcer, "he tried. That's   39
the big thing. He tried to do the best he could with what God gave him. He should get a nice raise for trying so hard."

"Ladies and gentlemen—" said the ballerina, reading the bulletin.   40
She must have been extraordinarily beautiful, because the mask she wore was hideous. And it was easy to see that she was the strongest and most graceful of all the dancers, for her handicap bags were as big as those worn by two-hundred-pound men.

And she had to apologize at once for her voice, which was a very   41
unfair voice for a woman to use. Her voice was a warm, luminous, timeless melody. "Excuse me—" she said, and she began again, making her voice absolutely uncompetitive.

"Harrison Bergeron, age fourteen," she said in a grackle squawk,   42
"has just escaped from jail, where he was held on suspicion of plotting to overthrow the government. He is a genius and an athlete, is under-handicapped, and should be regarded as extremely dangerous."

A police photograph of Harrison Bergeron was flashed on the   43
screen—upside down, then sideways, upside down again, then right side up. The picture showed the full length of Harrison against a background calibrated in feet and inches. He was exactly seven feet tall.

The rest of Harrison's appearance was Halloween and hardware.   44
Nobody had ever borne heavier handicaps. He had outgrown hindrances faster than the H-G men could think them up. Instead of a little ear radio for a mental handicap, he wore a tremendous pair of earphones, and spectacles with thick wavy lenses. The spectacles were to make him not only half blind, but to give him whanging headaches besides.

Scrap metal was hung all over him. Ordinarily, there was a certain   45
symmetry, a military neatness to the handicaps issued to strong people, but Harrison looked like a walking junkyard. In the race of life, Harrison carried three hundred pounds.

And to offset his good looks, the H-G men required that he wear at   46
all times a red rubber ball for a nose, keep his eyebrows shaved off, and cover his even white teeth with black caps at snaggle-tooth random.

"If you see this boy," said the ballerina, "do not—I repeat, do   47
not—try to reason with him."

There was a shriek of a door being torn from its hinges.   48

Screams and barking cries of consternation came from the tele-   49
vision set. The photograph of Harrison Bergeron on the screen
jumped again and again, as though dancing to the tune of an earthquake.

George Bergeron correctly identified the earthquake, and well he   50
might have—for many was the time his own home had danced to the
same crashing tune. "My God—" said George, "that must be
Harrison!"

The realization was blasted from his mind instantly by the sound   51
of an automobile collision in his head.

When George could open his eyes again, the photograph of   52
Harrison was gone. A living, breathing Harrison filled the screen.

Clanking, clownish, and huge, Harrison stood in the center of the   53
studio. The knob of the uprooted studio door was still in his hand.
Ballerinas, technicians, musicians, and announcers cowered on their
knees before him, expecting to die.

"I am the Emperor!" cried Harrison. "Do you hear? I am the   54
Emperor! Everybody must do what I say at once!" He stamped his
foot and the studio shook.

"Even as I stand here—" he bellowed, "crippled, hobbled, sick-   55
ened—I am a greater ruler than any man who ever lived! Now watch
me become what I *can* become!"

Harrison tore the straps of his handicap harness like wet tissue   56
paper, tore straps guaranteed to support five thousand pounds.

Harrison's scrap-iron handicaps crashed to the floor.   57

Harrison thrust his thumbs under the bar of the padlock that   58
secured his head harness. The bar snapped like celery. Harrison
smashed his headphones and spectacles against the wall.

He flung away his rubber-ball nose, revealed a man that would   59
have awed Thor, the god of Thunder.

"I shall now select my Empress!" he said, looking down on the   60
cowering people. "Let the first woman who dares rise to her feet
claim her mate and her throne!"

A moment passed, and then a ballerina arose, swaying like a willow. 61

Harrison plucked the mental handicap from her ear, snapped off 62
her physical handicaps with marvelous delicacy. Last of all, he
removed her mask.

She was blindingly beautiful! 63

"Now—said Harrison, taking her hand, "shall we show the peo- 64
ple the meaning of the word dance? Music!" he commanded.

The musicians scrambled back into their chairs, and Harrison 65
stripped them of their handicaps, too. "Play your best," he told them,
"and I'll make you barons and dukes and earls."

The music began. It was normal at first—cheap, silly, false. But 66
Harrison snatched two musicians from their chairs, waved them like
batons as he sang the music he wanted played. He slammed them
back into their chairs.

The music began again and was much improved. 67

Harrison and his Empress merely listened to the music for a while— 68
listened gravely, as though synchronizing their heartbeats with it.

They shifted their weights to their toes. 69

Harrison placed his big hands on the girl's tiny waist, letting her 70
sense the weightlessness that would soon be hers.

And then, in an explosion of joy and grace, into the air they 71
sprang!

Not only were the laws of the land abandoned, but the law of 72
gravity and the laws of motion as well.

They reeled, whirled, swiveled, flounced, capered, gamboled, and 73
spun.

They leaped like deer on the moon. 74

The studio ceiling was thirty feet high, but each leap brought the 75
dancers nearer to it.

It became their obvious intention to kiss the ceiling. 76

They kissed it. 77

And then, neutralizing gravity with love and pure will, they 78
remained suspended in air inches below the ceiling, and they kissed
each other for a long, long time.

It was then that Diana Moon Glampers, the Handicapper General, 79
came into the studio with a double-barreled ten-gauge shotgun. She

fired twice, and the Emperor and Empress were dead before they hit the floor.

Diana Moon Glampers loaded the gun again. She aimed at the musicians and told them they had ten seconds to get their handicaps back on.   80

It was then that the Bergerons' television tube burned out.   81

Hazel turned to comment about the blackout to George. But George had gone to the kitchen for a can of beer.   82

George came back in with the beer, paused while a handicap signal shook him. And then he sat down again. "You been crying?" he said to Hazel.   83

"Yup," she said.   84

"What about?" he said.   85

"I forget," she said. "Something real sad on television."   86

"What was it?" he said.   87

"It's all kind of mixed up in my mind," said Hazel.   88

"Forget sad things," said George.   89

"I always do," said Hazel.   90

"That's my girl," said George. He winced. There was the sound of a riveting gun in his head.   91

"Gee—I could tell that one was a doozy," said Hazel.   92

"You can say that again," said George.   93

"Gee—I could tell that one was a doozy."   94

Focusing on the Story

1. Amendments are additions or corrections of errors. What do the 211th, 212th, and 213th Amendments to the Constitution do? What is the job of the United States Handicapper General and her agents?
2. Why is Harrison in jail? What crimes has he committed? And why can't George and Hazel think about it very hard?
3. Why is George required to wear "a little mental handicap radio in his ear"? Why do the ballerinas have to wear different weights and ugly masks? Who has to wear the most hideous mask? Why doesn't Hazel have to wear handicaps?
4. Why do all the announcers have speech impediments? What are the criteria for salary raises and rewards in 2081?

5. When Harrison Bergeron appears on television, he looks like "Halloween and hardware." What does this mean? Describe Harrison as he appears on television, and briefly summarize the ending of the story.

Interpreting and Evaluating

1. When George says that "pretty soon we'd be right back to the dark ages," to what time is he referring? What did people do then that was so terrible?
2. Vonnegut uses many colorful words in his story. Point out two or three examples. What effect do such vivid verbs, strong nouns, adjectives, and adverbs have on the story as a whole?
3. Even though the setting is the year 2081, Kurt Vonnegut, Jr., is obviously commenting on our own society in this story. What is he criticizing? Does he think absolute equality is ideal, or does he think that competition is healthy? Is his tone mocking or serious?
4. Descartes, a seventeenth-century French philosopher, said, "I think; therefore I am" (or I exist). How is the ability to think related to our existence as human beings? What will happen to a society in which people are not allowed to think and express their thoughts?
5. Is advancement of human knowledge possible without competition? How would our democratic institutions fare if no value was placed on human intelligence and thought?

Ideas For Writing and Further Discussion

1. What would an ideal society look like in your opinion? What would the ideal government do? What qualities would people possess in an ideal society? What qualities would they lack? Write an essay in which you discuss several aspects of an ideal society. You may organize your essay around answers to some of the above questions. Suggested *thesis*: three or four aspects of an ideal society such as what the government would do, the qualities people would possess, and the qualities they would lack.
   Each *body paragraph* should explore one aspect of the thesis and show how it would contribute to an ideal society.

2. As a basic principle of a democracy, we believe that all people are born equal. What does this statement mean? Does it mean equality before the law only? Does being born equal mean that all people have to remain equal? Write an essay in which you explore the meaning of the statement that all people are born equal.
   Suggested *thesis*: two or three interpretations of the statement that all people are born equal.
   Each *body paragraph* should explore one such interpretation and give examples that illustrate it.

Text Credits

Allende, Isabel "The Schoolteacher's Guest" from *The Stories of Eva Luna* by Isabel Allende. Translated from Spanish by Margaret Sayers Peden. Copyright © 1989 by Isabel Allende. English translation © 1991 by Macmillan Publishing Company. Reprinted by permission of Scribner, a division of Simon & Schuster.

Angelou, Maya "Mary" from *I Know Why the Caged Bird Sings,* pages 101–108. Copyright © 1969 and renewed 1997 by Maya Angelou. Reprinted by permission of Random House, Inc.

Buchwald, Art "Fresh Air Will Kill You" from *Have I Ever Lied to You* by Art Buchwald. Copyright ©1968 by Art Buchwald. Used by permission of G.P. Putnam's Sons, a division of Penguin Group (USA) Inc.

Caldwell, Erskine "Horse Thief" from *Vanity Fair,* November 1933. Copyright © 1933 Conde Nast Publications Inc. and renewed © 1960 by Erskine Caldwell.

Chekhov, Anton "The Confession" from *Anton Chekhov: Selected Stories* by Anton Chekhov. Copyright © 1960 by Ann Dunnigan. By permission of Dutton Signet, a division of Penguin Putnam, Inc.

Chekhov (1860–1904)

De Maupassant, Guy "The Necklace" from *The Collected Novels and Short Stories of Guy de Maupassant* by Guy de Maupassant, translated by Ernest Boyd. Copyright © 1922 and renewed ©1952 by Alfred A. Knopf, Inc. Reprinted by permission of Alfred A. Knopf, a division of Random House, Inc.

Dixon, Dr. Roland (recorded by) "Butterfly Man" by the Maidu Indians, from *The Inland Whale* by Theodora Kroeber. Copyright © 1959, reprinted by permission of Indiana University Press, Bloomington.

Heker, Liliana "The Stolen Party" from *Other Fires: Short Fiction by Latin American Women* edited and translated by Alberto Manguel. Copyright © 1982 by Liliana Heker. Translation ©1986 by Alberto Manguel. Reprinted by permission of Crown Publishers, Inc., a division of Random House, Inc. and Westwood Creative Artists, Ltd.

Hemingway, Ernest "Old Man at the Bridge" from *The Short Stories of Ernest Hemingway.* Copyright © 1938 by Ernest Hemingway. Renewed © 1966 by Mary Hemingway. Reprinted with permission of Scribner, a division of Simon & Schuster Adult Publishing Group.

Hughes. Langston "Thank You M'am" from *Short Stories* by Langston Hughes. Copyright © 1996 by Ramona Bass and Arnold Rampersad. Reprinted by permission of Hill and Wang, a division of Farrar, Straus and Giroux, LLC.

Jackson, Shirley "Charles" from *The Lottery and Other Stories* by Shirley Jackson. Copyright © 1948, 1949 by Shirley Jackson and renewed © 1976, 1977 by Laurence Hyman, Barry Hyman, Mrs. Sarah Webster, and Mrs. Joanne Schurer. Reprinted by permission of Farrar, Straus & Giroux, LLC.

Jen, Gish "A Boy with His Hat Over His Crotch" from *Typical American* by Gish Jen, copyright © 1991. Reprinted by permission of Houghton Mifflin Co. All rights reserved.

Kantor, MacKinlay "A Man Who Had No Eye," copyright ©1931 by Liberty.